Innovations in Legal KM

EDITED BY HARRY LAWRENCE

Commissioning editor
Alex Davies

Editorial assistant
Harry Lawrence

Published by
Globe Law and Business Ltd
3 Mylor Close
Horsell
Woking
Surrey GU21 4DD
United Kingdom
Tel: +44 20 3745 4770
www.globelawandbusiness.com

ISBN: 978-1-78358-312-6
A catalogue record for this book is available from the British Library

Contents

Executive summary

The discipline of knowledge management (KM) continues to evolve along with our ability to record larger and more varied kinds of information than ever before. Since its inception in the 1990s, it has passed through several stages, quickly becoming a credible field, and now an integral part of major businesses worldwide. Now, many have started to argue that KM is undergoing resurgence, possibly even transforming into KM 3.0, thanks to developments in artificial intelligence (AI). And, while AI has been around for many years, it has become a buzzword in the industry as questions loom over what it could mean for the labor market of the future.

Adoption has been relatively slow in the legal profession, owing in part to its conservative nature, individual-focused training and no real incentive to overhaul the hourly billing model.[1] When in-house legal teams can exceed 1,000 people, sharing and reusing knowledge can easily become inefficient, with counsel often needlessly paying for the same research twice. Global intelligence software leader Comintelli estimates that $8.5 billion per year is lost between Fortune 500 companies alone on poor KM,[2] up from $31.5 billion in 2004,[3] suggesting a recent rise in the number of firms embracing the concept.

Despite this, there are still challenges posed to the legal world, and sharing insight is more vital than ever, not only within companies but between them. *Innovations in Legal KM* explores the endeavors of various legal firms – the problems they have faced, and the solutions they have developed – to improve their KM processes, and, ultimately, their bottom line.

This book is divided into nine chapters, each one a case study focusing on a specific area of KM in practice. In chapter one, Hélène Russell, founder of TheKnowledgeBusiness, reminds us that KM projects aren't always easy to measure. In her case study, she simplifies this task by highlighting how to understand your purpose in measuring, the audience for whom you are measuring, and the practicalities of measuring for an accurate result.

Oz Benamram reflects on how White & Case became a hostage in a vendor relationship and used innovation to find a solution in chapter two. With reference to the suppliers of legal information and change management, Benamram describes how White & Case has optimized its research tools to deliver value through increased efficiency and – interestingly – reduction of costs to clients.

In a similar vein, Jack Bostelman, president of KM/JD Consulting LLC, and Chris Boyd, senior director of professional services at Wilson Sonsini Goodrich & Rosati LLP, outline in chapter three how implementing KM projects into a firm can increase profitability and create more value from work undertaken. Using a base case model, they show how a firm's financial figures can be improved with three kinds of KM project, proving that a rethink of a lawyer's day-to-day practice can have realistic financial benefits.

"How do you fix something that no one thinks is broken?" So asks Cynthia L. Brown, recognizing the endemic problem facing law firms. The solution to this problem need not come in the form of huge, firmwide changes. In chapter four, she introduces Littler Mendelson's Knowledge Desk, a centralized system designed to consolidate attorneys' questions, increase the efficiency of its internal KM and similar departments, free up time for higher-level projects, and – most importantly – better serve its attorneys.

In chapter five, Mark Gediman, of Best Best & Krieger LLP, explores how a law firm library can effectively utilize KM to help deal with partner requests. Using a real-world example of a request for a specialized repository of documents, Gediman runs through the key areas of information that KM has to offer, and how they can be leveraged to effectively respond to a partner's request.

Andrea Miskolczi of Wolf Theiss tackles the problem of the industry itself: lawyers are taught not to like collaboration and silo themselves away. Using research from Dr. Heidi Gardner PhD, a Distinguished Fellow in the Center on the Legal Profession at Harvard Law School, Andrea Miskolczi looks at the barriers to and benefits of smart collaboration in chapter six, and what steps can be taken to break down those silos.

It is easy to forget that a firm's size can have such a huge impact on its resources, and therefore its departments. Harriet Creamer talks about the way forward for smaller and medium-sized companies in chapter seven, advocating a lawyer-led KM model, where resourcing is largely focused on lawyers, rather than dedicated KM resources.

In chapter eight, Cyndi Murphy gives a detailed walkthrough of how Stewart McKelvey has begun to leverage its data. It has taken advantage of tools such as a reduced and more consistent taxonomy, a centralized user interface that's easy to use and an added versatility to that system so that old data can be used in new ways. Now with SMartNet, the company's centralized document management system, it can feedback in real time and continue to utilize matter-centric KM.

James Loft, CEO at Aigen, looks at value within organizations and how they approach problems and seize opportunities in complex working environments. The concept of 'value' is perhaps taken for granted nowadays; in chapter nine, James draws a clear picture of what value is in relation to certain technologies, and how that can be used to make new knowledge from old, scale automated decision-making, increase specialization, and support those working environments with the best possible knowledge.

References

1. Lamont, J., "AI takes hold in the legal profession", January 2017. See: http://www.kmworld.com/Articles/Editorial/Features/AI-takes-hold-in-the-legal-profession-115913.aspx
2. Are you suffering from Infobesity? (2017, September 21). Retrieved from: https://comintelli.com/are-you-suffering-from-infobesity/
3. Babcock, P., "Shedding Light on Knowledge Management", May 2004. See: https://www.shrm.org/hr-today/news/hr-magazine/Pages/0504covstory.aspx

About the authors

Oz Benamram is chief knowledge officer at White & Case, providing the firm with strategic direction on the use of KM and technology. He leads the knowledge department in developing and implementing the systems and processes that enable the firm to use its collective knowledge to benefit clients worldwide.

Oz is a globally recognized thought leader and a frequent speaker on legal IT and KM subjects. He has won numerous awards for leading innovation in legal KM, including the creation of an enterprise search system.

Jack Bostelman is president of KM/JD Consulting LLC in San Francisco, California, which advises law firm leaders on practice management, including knowledge management and other productivity improvements. Before founding KM/JD Consulting, Jack was a partner for over 20 years at pre-eminent AmLaw 20 firm Sullivan & Cromwell in New York City, where he had a nationally recognized transactional securities law practice and exercised management responsibilities.

Chris Boyd is senior director of professional services at Wilson Sonsini Goodrich & Rosati LLP in Palo Alto, California. Chris runs the firm's recruiting, training, and knowledge management programs, all of which are designed to help the firm deliver superlative value to its clients. Chris was previously an attorney at the firm and also led KM programs at several internet start-ups.

Cynthia L. Brown is the director of research services at Littler Mendelson, the world's largest employment and labor law practice representing management where she has bridged the worlds of the Library and Knowledge Management since 2007.

Her previous experience includes working as in-house counsel for four years at a small risk management firm, as an account manager and training consultant at LexisNexis, and running a solo library in Salt Lake City at Jones Waldo Holbrook & McDonough.

Harriet Creamer has over 25 years of experience of working in the legal services sector, both as a client lawyer and in management. Harriet trained, practiced and became a partner at Freshfields Bruckhaus Derringer, where – having become the City of London's first PSL – she headed up their knowledge management function, developing and managing knowledge services across their worldwide network of offices. Since leaving Freshfields, Harriet has been a director of Outer Circle, a consultancy she established with a colleague to provide knowledge management and practice development advice, principally to professional services firms. She has extensive experience of helping firms use their knowledge strategically, both to strengthen client relationships and drive profitability.

She also advises firms on how to ensure that their knowledge management activities are aligned to and support the delivery of their strategic business objectives and that they derive value from their investment in knowledge management. She regularly works with partners and groups of partners to help them identify and prioritize the development of key knowledge tools for their practice areas.

Harriet is an experienced presenter and a regular speaker at KM conferences and other events, as well as writing regularly on aspects of KM for the legal press. She is a member of the Law Society's Standing Committee on Company Law.

Mark Gediman is the director of information services for Best Best & Krieger LLP and has been with the firm since 2000, managing the research needs of more than 200 attorneys and paralegals in nine offices from DC to California. He is a past president of the Southern California Association of Law Libraries (SCALL) and the cofounder and cochair of the Competitive Intelligence Caucus of the Private Law Libraries-Information Professionals (PLL-IP) of the American Association of Law Libraries (AALL).

He has over 25 years of experience in law library management and writes regularly on competitive intelligence, research, and library management issues. He presents frequently for AALL and the Inland Counties Association of Paralegals as well as for SCALL, NoCALL, ACI and HALL. He has authored articles in *AALL Spectrum*, *Practicing Law Management Week*, *Paralegal Today*, and *Facts & Findings – The Magazine of the National Association of Legal Assistants* (NALA). He is a graduate of the University of California, Riverside.

James Loft is a graduate of knowledge management from Loughborough University and has worked extensively in innovation and new technologies in transport and financial services culminating in the running of an artificial intelligence consultancy firm that helps companies make AI tools fit their businesses rather than the other way around. His mission is to demystify the world of 'applied AI' for organizations, to level the playing field for the progression of the technology now, rather than as a vision for the future.

With an experienced background in innovation and service design, he understands the gentle but vital balance between design and technology, and advocates an MVP style approach to new technology in order to achieve success. An active member of a community of AI companies, tools and platforms, James possesses a broad understanding of the possibilities the technologies can offer and will support in their implementation where possible to advance the marketplace.

Andrea Miskolczi is the chief business development and marketing officer at Wolf Theiss. Her extensive international experience in the legal market ranges from legal advisory experience at Linklaters to devising market-leading business development and marketing strategies at Wolf Theiss. Andrea has a proven track record in planning and directing business development and marketing programs to boost client growth and attract new mandates. She manages the firm's CRM and marketing activities as well as public relations efforts, enhancing the Wolf Theiss brand identity.

With a background in project management, Andrea is skilled at driving large-scale cross-border organizational development projects that have been recognized by The *Financial Times* Innovative Lawyer Awards among others. For instance, she developed and implemented the Wolf Theiss School of Excellence, a firm-wide cohesive, standardized training program, and launched the firm's initiative to foster "smart collaboration".

She is passionate about having a strategic approach towards fostering innovation and is an alumnus of a Harvard Business School course on this topic ('Disruptive Strategy with Clayton Christensen').

Cyndi Murphy is the knowledge manager in the Halifax, Nova Scotia office of Stewart McKelvey. Her firmwide responsibilities include liaising with various administrative departments for the successful implementation of knowledge management projects, overseeing content management of the internal Sharepoint portal and various internal research-oriented databases, and attending meetings of the Practice Innovation Advisory Committee.

She was a member of the three-person team that designed and implemented a new Sharepoint portal that launched in January 2016 and she continues to be integrally involved with ongoing enhancements to the portal. Cyndi is a former president of the Canadian Association of Law Libraries and an active member of the association's Knowledge Management and Private Law Libraries Special Interest Groups.

Hélène Russell of TheKnowledgeBusiness specializes in helping organizations to grow and improve profitability, by helping them to understand and improve their knowledge systems. Hélène is the author of the Law Society's *Knowledge Management Handbook* and Legal Monitor's *Practical Projects in Legal KM*. She teaches open and in-house courses in knowledge management and also offers coaching, mentoring, and advice. She also runs Knowledge Network UK, the only regional knowledge sharing and networking group for law firm KMers in the UK.

Hélène has spoken extensively on KM for ARK, Butterworths, UWE, Bristol Law Society, Allice, and at Knowledge Network UK, and has written regularly for *Managing Partner* magazine. After a decade as a solicitor with a major regional firm specializing in clinical negligence defense litigation, eight years in knowledge management and having recently obtained an MBA with distinction, she has a unique, deep understanding of how knowledge flow helps law firms and professional services organizations.

Kathy Skinner is director of research and information services at White & Case. In her role, Kathy leads the global research and information team as port of the firm's broader knowledge function, and she is responsible for the coordination and delivery of research services and products, along with ensuring operational excellence and cost-efficiency in all of the firms' 41 offices.

Prior to joining White & Case, Kathy was director of research services at Morrison and Foerster. Kathy received her A.B. and M.L.I.S. degrees from the University of California at Berkeley.

Chapter 1:
Measurement of KM projects: a practical guide for busy people

By Hélène Russell, TheKnowledgeBusiness, founder

This chapter looks at the measurement of knowledge projects and activities in a simple, practical way, with the aim of helping busy individuals understand whether their various knowledge management (KM) projects and activities are having a positive effect and are value for money in a general sense. Be forewarned: the benefits of KM are often intangible and the way that KM affects tangibles can be complex, so measurement is difficult. That doesn't, however, mean that you can't approximate an answer which is useful within a business setting.

The value and difficulty of measuring

There are many different ways that knowledge artifacts and flows can benefit organizations (see Figure 1).

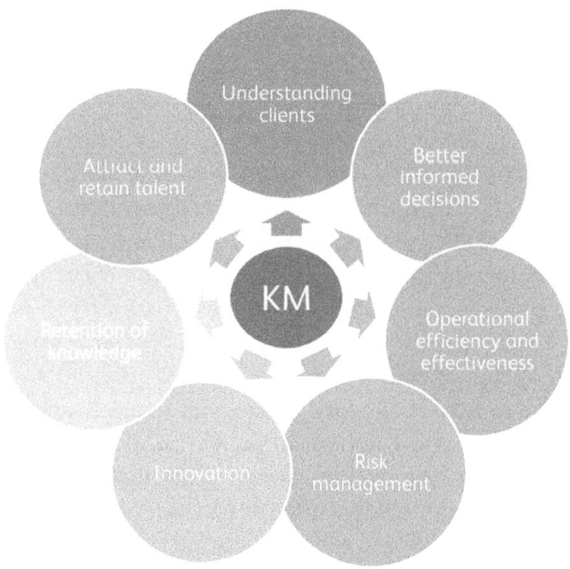

Figure 1: The benefits of KM

Measuring the numbers of knowledge artifacts or activities is not usually difficult. You could probably easily find out how many articles you have in your organization's database or how many training meetings took place last month. The difficulty lies in understanding how those artifacts and activities are acting on your organization to help or hinder it in its goals, understanding the quality of those knowledge artifacts and activities, and whether they provide a good return on investment.

When considering the effect of artifacts and activities, there are usually many complex factors at play. X does not simply cause Y. The effects of a single knowledge project are intricately entwined with other business systems and affected by serendipitous events and events outside the organization's control.

For example, a lawyer is mulling over a complex issue and is planning to look at the firm's knowledge bank before drafting a complex document. He decides to get a coffee first. Whilst making his coffee he chats to another lawyer and discovers that she has recently dealt with the same issue, researched it intensively, and found a neat solution which her client was delighted with. This is clearly a successful knowledge activity or interaction: the first lawyer gets the right information and knowledge quickly and easily, and finds a solution which is likely to please his client. What, however, would be measured and what would this interaction tell us about this law firm's KM systems? Nothing would be recorded in any database viewing or download figures and it may not be recalled by either lawyer during an annual knowledge survey or discussion about culture and networks. Is this a success for the knowledge-sharing culture, a failure of the knowledge database, neither, or both?

Similarly, when lawyers or other professionals are trying to understand whether it is more cost-effective to work in one way rather than another, perhaps deciding whether to impose a particular workflow or checklist, this may have a more complicated result than a simple change in billings or profits (see Figure 2). There could be lower chargeable hours per matter and lower billing levels in the short term, but, in the long term, higher quality advice, higher customer satisfaction, lower professional negligence claims, lower attrition rates, and more matters undertaken or higher profit fixed fees.

How well KM activities work in an organization depends greatly on its culture, history, and the dedication of the individuals involved, and factors outside the organization's control can have a significant effect.

Although it is undoubtedly difficult to value "knowledge" and knowledge activities and systems, the pragmatic truth is that those who run

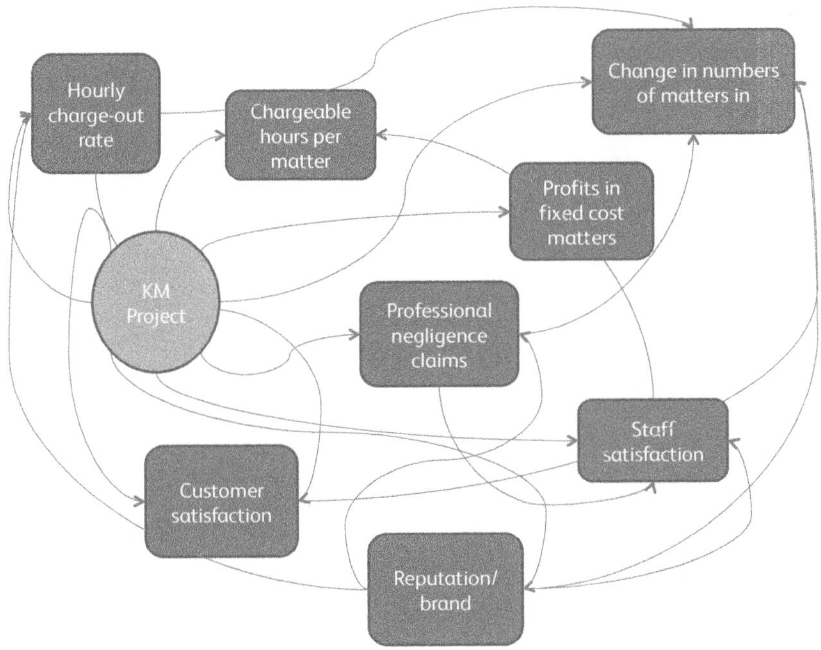

Figure 2: The effects of KM projects

organizations need to understand what return on investment they will get for their spending on KM, which projects or schemes ought to be rolled out more widely, and which projects or activities should be changed.

Where to start with KM measurement

I recommend, when planning your measurement system, you use the following process (see Figure 3 for the full process):

1. **Why** – understand your **purpose** in measuring;
2. **Who** – understand your **audience** for the measurement; and
3. **How** – understand the **practicalities** of measuring for an accurate result

Also keep in mind these two truisms:

- "What is measured gets managed" – what is measured within a business tends to get noticed and improved. Things that aren't measured often languish on the "to do" pile.

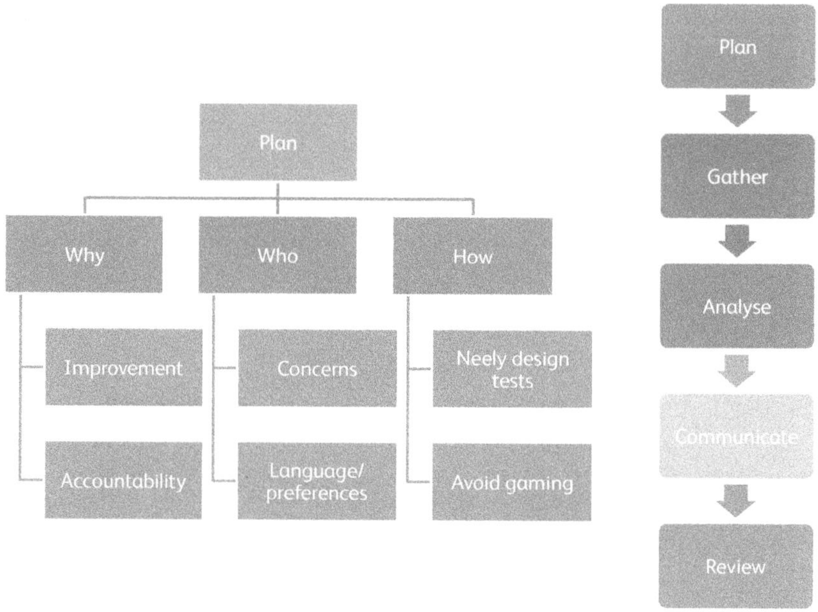

Figure 3: How to create and use measurement systems in KM

- "You get what you measure" – measurement itself can have unexpected and negative results, with employees focusing on improving figures themselves rather than the business case behind those measurements.

Why: understanding your purpose

Your first task is to understand your purpose:

- Why do you need this measurement?
- What is the business benefit of knowing this answer?
- What are you going to do with the results?

You need to take the appropriate level of measurements to inform and support your decision-making and action. There is no point in measurement for measurement's sake and too many measurements can be counterproductive, as they can create confusion. If you can't take action based on the measurement in relation to that KM project or activity, don't waste time and money on that aspect (unless you are gathering evidence for a known future action).

If you are unsure whether your measurement is actionable, ask yourself whether you want the measurement to go up, down, or stay flat. If you don't know which way you want the measurement to go, or don't know what you will do in each situation, the measurement is not actionable and you need to think again.

Common reasons for measuring KM activities are:

- Improvement or quality; and
- Judgment or accountability.

For example, most KMers will be measuring to find out:

- If their actions are adding value to the organization;
- If an investment in a particular project or KM activity is good value for money;
- Whether or not a particular implementation is on track, a particular approach is working, or to identify gaps in their approach;
- Whether they should expand a pilot KM project or shelve it;
- Where a project doesn't appear to be working, whether that is an inherent problem and that that project is unlikely ever to work within their organization, or whether it can be put back on track with a few tweaks;
- What their users' or stakeholders' natural modes of working are, in order to design KM activities which suit them and will be adopted easily;
- Whether their stakeholders are fulfilling their part of the KM bargain or not, and – if not – how the system can be adapted to encourage more participation; and
- To identify the key barriers to engagement.

Your "purpose" for measuring will drive the development of your measurement systems.

Given how difficult it is to understand the effect of KM activities and projects on business outcomes (see Figure 2), I recommend that you take a balance of measurements. The complexity of your measurement system will depend upon the size and nature of the project and budget, but I recommend that, even for a small project, you at least include qualitative and quantitative, and leading and lagging elements. Whether you measure across all four perspectives of the Balanced Scorecard depends on the project and its budget. Too many measurements are as unhelpful as too few.

The Balanced Scorecard

The Balanced Scorecard was first proposed by Kaplan and Norton in 1992[1] and updated in 2000[2] and is one of the most influential business ideas in relation to business drivers over the last 75 years. They understood that traditional financial accounting measures, such as earnings per share and return on investment can give misleading signals and negatively affect a business' ability to innovate and improve continuously.[3]

The Balanced Scorecard emphasizes a simple but balanced perspective, using a handful of hard and soft measures and leading and lagging indicators, built around four key areas, asking four basic questions:

1. How do customers see us? (customer perspective);
2. What must we excel at? (internal business perspective);
3. Can we continue to improve and create value? (innovation, knowledge, and learning perspective); and
4. How do we look financially, to shareholders? (financial stewardship perspective).

It aims to act like "dials in a cockpit" so that managers can take in complex information from all four perspectives at a glance, and, ensuring that improvements in one area (say, financial) are not at the expense of other areas (say, customer perspective or innovation or learning), keep the organization on track against its strategy. It is the "hands down favorite" of Dr. Melissie Rumizen, author of *The Complete Idiot's Guide to Knowledge Management*.[4]

The Balanced Scorecard also blends "looking back" and "looking forward" to keep organizations on track. It is fairly easy to measure what has happened in the past. This will tell you whether or not what you have done in the past has worked or not, but it won't tell you whether what you are currently doing will be a success.

"Looking back" measures are "lagging indicators" and are output measures, such as changes to profitability, and tell you what has already happened.

"Looking forward" measures are "leading indicators" and are input measures, such as the ongoing costs (of staff, of IT) and activity measures such as level of participation (web page views, amount of activity on a wiki), and give you "early warning" of what might happen.

"Leading" and "lagging" are not absolute notions. Leading is upstream in a work process. Lagging is downstream in the same process. A particular measurement can be upstream when measuring one aspect, downstream for another, and some measurements can be difficult to categorize. Both leading and lagging factors can be quantitative or qualitative.

For example, if you work in a knowledge-intensive firm and you would like to trial a change to a training and learning program by swapping from in-person training lunches based on lectures to online videos and quizzes, you could wait until the program has run its course, had a positive or negative effect on the knowledgeability of your staff, and led to a measurable change in numbers of clients and profitability, or you could take leading measurements to give you early warning if the program isn't working. Leading measurements in this case could include the numbers of people taking, finishing, or passing the online courses. If the numbers of people wanting to start the course drops, perhaps word has spread that people do not feel the courses are worth investing time in? If people are keen to start and finish, but fail the quizzes, you will get an early warning that something is not right with the content or delivery of the knowledge.

Who: understanding the audience for the measurement

It doesn't really matter how sound your data[5] is if you cannot communicate the results in a way that is persuasive for those who need to take action.

Common audiences for the measurement are:

- Those running KM activities or projects;
- Users, stakeholders, or communities your KM activities/projects serve; and
- Managers and directors at various levels in the organization, and those who allocate resources.

Once you've clarified your audience, you need to ask yourself: "For the purpose I've identified, what does this audience care about?"

Concentrate on the measurements or KPIs within the four Balanced Scorecard perspectives that your audience cares particularly about. You can look at financial stewardship in a number of ways, but your senior managers probably have a favorite measurement they always take notice of. No matter how great you think your measurements are, if they don't persuade those who need to take action, they haven't fulfilled their purpose.

If you are uncertain about a particular audience's preferences, ask them. This isn't a matter of "sexing up" data to mislead. It is about avoiding wasting time measuring one aspect when a different but similar one would have a more persuasive effect on that audience. Even if their preferred measurement isn't the perfect one in your opinion, still use it. It has the benefit of being established and authoritative to your audience. If you really can't use it, explain how your measurements link to it.

For example, you are measuring to demonstrate that a particular discrete KM project is making a significant difference to profitability and ought to be rolled out more widely and your audience is senior managers.

Ask yourself:

- What do those senior managers care about? What keeps them up at night?
- What data have they previously taken notice of?
- What "language" do they listen to and speak?

The senior managers may worry about profitability, levels of innovation when new competitors enter their market, or key staff attrition after a merger, depending on what is happening in the organization at the time. They may be mainly from a financial background and take notice of short-term share price changes or profit per equity partner. They may care most about market position and client satisfaction surveys. They may care greatly about efficiency and effectiveness.

Alternatively, if you are using a measurement to help you understand whether a smaller KM project appears to be a good use of your own limited time, you may focus on measurements which you personally find compelling. For example, you think a project relating to serendipitous conversation will improve trusting networks and person-to-person knowledge sharing. It isn't a complex, expensive, unpopular or onerous project, so you may want to minimize the cost of measurement and focus on a simple one-off qualitative measurement, such as a survey or focus group. Once you are satisfied that the project appears to be working and is worth rolling out further, you may widen measurements across the four Balanced Scorecard perspectives to ensure that there are no unanticipated negative results that could steer your organization off-course and which will include measurements meaningful for the new audience, who may not be persuaded by a focus group discussion, but may be persuaded by a reduction in early notification of potential professional negligence claims or an increase in client satisfaction measurements in relation to knowledgeability of staff.

Try, where possible, to gather stories that illustrate your data, as well as the data itself. While an increase in general client satisfaction measurements may be compelling, hearing the audio file of the actual interview with a client expressing in their own words how the knowledgeability of staff persuaded them to place more orders is even more compelling.

How: deciding on the practicalities of measurement

Once you are clear on the purpose of your measurement and its audience, you will need to decide on the practicalities. Your measurements should be reliable and valid and, for larger projects, you should spell out your methodology in detail.

You need to be clear about:

- What measurements are you going to take? How are you going to take them?
- Who will collect the data?
- How, when, and how often will they collect it?

You will also need to consider how much you can afford to spend on measurement. Some measurements will be collected in any event, so are low in cost (although don't forget that you'll still need to analyze the results) and some will cost money to arrange, collect and analyze. The nature of your KM project and its potential to affect your organization will determine your budget for measurement.

As you are only measuring to take action in relation to your KM project and activities, you need to have a trustworthy baseline from which to note changes. You must also ensure you take the same measurements in the same way before and after the change for the results to be reliable ("comparing apples with apples").

A balance of measurements (using qualitative and quantitative, leading and lagging, across the four facets of the Balanced Scorecard) can get us closer to understanding what is happening as a result of our activities and overcoming the difficulties previously outlined. It will also help us to even out any gaming[6] (see page 11).

User surveys are extremely valuable for qualitative research, but can't be used too often because of user fatigue. Surveys can include both qualitative and quantitative elements and can focus on one project or activity or combine questions about a number of them. Where you would like to distil an opinion into an easily comparable figure, I recommend using a Likert Scale (where your respondents rate their response from 1 to 5, 1 being "strongly disagree" and 5 being "strongly agree"). There is more advice on how to write a good survey at Annex 4. Informal discussions are just as important as formal soundings, so also get to know what people think by talking to them.

At this point, I recommend that you take a moment to read and understand the 10 measurement design tests (Figure 4 and Annex 2) described by Professor Andrew Neely, head of the Institute of Manufacturing at Cambridge and expert in designing KPIs and measuring business performance.

Neely Design Tests

1. The truth test
2. The focus test
3. The relevancy test
4. The consistency test
5. The access test
6. The clarity test
7. The so-what test
8. The timeliness test
9. The cost test
10. The gaming test

Figure 4: The Neely Design Tests

While not all KM projects will be sufficiently large to warrant measurements that fulfil all these design tests, they are a great checklist to ensure that:

- You measure only what is necessary and relevant at the time that it is needed;
- Your measurements are the easiest and cheapest measurements to take, and remain consistent whoever gathers the data;
- You continue to measure only what you set out to measure; and

- You need to understand what is truly important to the firm to ensure that you concentrate on the right aspects. Once you have your data, remember that all measurements are not equal in value: "non-chargeable time saved" within a law firm is unlikely to be more important than quality, firm reputation or new business won, unless the changes are sizeable.

Unintended consequences and "gaming"

Measurement systems can cause distortions and unexpected consequences, particularly where they are linked to performance. These distortions can be conscious or subconscious, as people change their behavior to meet the targets set for them or the measurement systems applied to them.

There are numerous examples of unintended consequences to measurement systems in everyday life: teachers teaching to the *test* for SATs, not to benefit pupils' needs, but to improve their school's ranking or avoid criticism by Ofsted; GPs refusing to book patients in for appointments at all, even when patients are happy to wait, so as not to breach government rules about patients waiting 48 hours for an appointment.

People are nearly always more intelligent than systems. Your users and particularly your subject matter experts are likely to spot any weaknesses in your measurement systems and work out how to "game" the results that affect them. Quantitative measurements are particularly susceptible to gaming and so should always be balanced with qualitative measurements.

For example, in a law firm, you decide to measure numbers of submissions to a KM database as part of your measurements to try to understand the value of that database and the knowledge-sharing attitude of your lawyers. You wish to promote knowledge sharing, so you also reward this, perhaps by noting it during annual appraisals. You find an annual spike of submissions shortly before performance reviews. Of course, this is not a problem if the quality is good, although it would be easier to manage if submissions were spread out throughout the year, but in truth, quality is unlikely to be good if "box ticking" is the motivator. The firm "gets what it measures," in that it emphasizes other aspects of profitability all year, then switches to "softer" aspects at appraisal time.

Gaming can be minimized by approaching measurement using a number of different angles and by keeping an eye out for unusual results or improvements in quantitative results which don't reflect an improvement in quality, or are not matched by qualitative comments.

Analysis of data

As part of this practical guide, I won't be delving deeply into statistical analysis. My own experience has been that, in most cases, only simple tools are needed. You are primarily looking for relationships and trends (i.e. when *x* happens, what happens to *y*?). You will usually just need percentages, averages, ratios, and divergence from the mean, median, or mode. If the picture you uncover appears to be more complex, I recommend you tap into your network for help from someone with the right data analysis skills.

Reporting results

No matter how carefully you collate your data, you will need to communicate your results in a compelling way for it to be persuasive.

- Engage with your audience's needs and wants;
- Give enough context so that people can understand the results;
- Include the human face to the figures – a story or anecdote will have impact on your audience; and
- Decide where and how to publicize the results. If you plan to release the results on to the intranet, who will see it? Do you want all the results available to everyone, or do you want a detailed version for the Executive Board and a slimmed down version for the whole organization? What state of mind will your audience be in when they receive your results? How can you maximize their understanding?

Updating your measurements

As you gain experience in measuring your KM projects or activities, you will need to revise and update your measurement system. You may find that some of the goals (the "Why", see page 4) need more work. Your organization will also grow, adapt to different customers, change its IT systems, etc. You will need to identify any overlapping measurements and simplify them. You will need to replace measurements that are proving to be unhelpful, or those that have become too costly to justify. You will learn which measurements work particularly well with which audiences. You will need to keep a delicate balance between keeping measurements the same (so you can identify trends over time, measuring apples against apples) and adapting to new circumstances, and simplifying and focusing your measurements.

I recommend that you revisit your measurements and the Neely design tests at suitable intervals, perhaps annually, and adapt the measurements as appropriate.

Summary

Use Figure 2 to help you plan and implement your measurement systems.

1. Define the business objectives of measurement and understand what success will look like;
2. Identify those being measured and the audience for the results – each stakeholder views KM and defines success differently;
3. Decide what data will be collected and how. Use Neely's measurement design tests to ensure your measurements are appropriate;
4. Analyze and communicate the measures in the language of your audience;
5. Take action in relation to business objectives based on the results;
6. Review your combination of measures to ensure the right balance of quantitative and qualitative, leading and lagging measurements, and adjust as your goals develop;
7. Keep under review unexpected consequences and "gaming" the system of measurement; and
8. Don't measure everything – focus on what's important.

Annex 1

The big list of potential ways to measure KM systems.

Quantitative:

1. System user statistics;
2. Hits on a webpage;
3. Load times of web pages;
4. Dwell times (how long a user stays on a page);
5. Numbers of unique users;
6. Repeat visitors to a page;
7. Usage of externally provided KM;
8. Percentage of total employees using a system;
9. Uses of a precedent or the precedent database;
10. Numbers of contributions to knowledge database;
11. Numbers of questions asked on a discussion forum;
12. Frequency of updates by users;
13. Numbers of active community members;
14. Frequency of AAR meetings;
15. Numbers of calls to Information Services professionals;
16. Numbers of queries raised and responded to;
17. Time taken to respond to queries;
18. Numbers of people trained in KM;
19. Numbers of KM champions or sponsors;
20. Training events prepared or attended;
21. Length of time devoted to certain activities (e.g. preparing tenders or client seminars);
22. Non-chargeable time recorded;
23. Speed of document production;
24. Time to create new knowledge;
25. Number of repeat complaints;
26. Professional indemnity insurance claims;
27. Number of identified experts;

28. Number of people active in Communities of Practice (COPs);
29. Number of new employees;
30. Level of staff retention;
31. Retention of key staff;
32. Numbers of clients lost to leaving staff;
33. Number of knowledge debriefs;
34. Number of knowledge stories;
35. Invitations to speak at conferences or seminars, etc.;
36. Number of publications in relevant literature;
37. Number of contacts with knowledge institutes;
38. Benchmarking against suppliers, customers and peer businesses;
39. KM budget availability;
40. Proportion of employees making new idea suggestions;
41. Time to develop new ideas;
42. Ratio of new ideas generated to new ideas implemented;
43. Percentage of sales earned with new knowledge;
44. Savings by knowledge re-use;
45. Support staff cost reductions;
46. Reduction in cost of quality;
47. Information maintenance costs;
48. KM IT tool outage levels;
49. Level of leverage within a department;
50. Percentage of profit from fixed fee work;
51. Utilization level within a department;
52. Realization levels within a department;
53. Change in ranking in expert Directories (such as Legal 500 or Chambers); and
54. Level of understanding of KM within business plan or KM vision.

Qualitative:
Could be measured by surveys (of users, of support staff, of supervisors), focus groups, consultations etc.

1. Ease of access;
2. Quality of document production (that is, fewer mistakes);
3. Ease of location of an expert;
4. User (both user and support staff) satisfaction;
5. Confidence in the systems (success stories);
6. Quality of contributions to knowledge databases;
7. Sharing and use of best practices;
8. Ease of employing quality staff;
9. General employee satisfaction (both user and support staff);
10. Tool availability;
11. Knowledge user complaints;
12. Knowledge user satisfaction;
13. Client satisfaction in quality of legal work;
14. Client satisfaction in supporting client-facing KM (portals, newsletters, seminars);
15. Perceived usefulness surveys – how KM tool helps users accomplish their objectives;
16. Effectiveness of sharing communities;
17. Perceived attitudes to failure; and
18. Perceived attitudes to knowledge hoarding or other barriers to knowledge sharing.

Annex 2
Ten Measure Design Tests[7]

1. The truth test – are we really measuring what we set out to measure?
2. The focus test – are we only measuring what we set out to measure?
3. The relevancy test – is it the right measure of the performance measure we want to track?
4. The consistency test – will the data always be collected in the same way whoever measures it?

5. The access test – is it easy to locate and capture the data needed to make the measurement?
6. The clarity test – is any ambiguity possible in interpreting the results?
7. The so-what test – can and will the data be acted upon?
8. The timeliness test – can the data be accessed rapidly and frequently enough for action?
9. The cost test – is the measure worth the cost of measurement?
10. The gaming test – is the measure likely to encourage undesirable or inappropriate behavior?

Annex 3

Survey checklist

Design

- Plenty of open space and clear formatting;
- Easy-to-read font;
- Reasonable total length or divided into sections; and
- Start with easy questions.

Questions

- Short and succinct;
- Free of jargon;
- Clear and specific; and
- More options than "yes" or "no" (i.e. a five-point Likert scale + "don't know").

Avoid

- Double negatives;
- Over-reliance on respondents' memories;
- Leading questions;
- Loaded questions;
- Double-barreled questions; and
- Splitting questions over two pages.

Annex 4
Example and template

Business goal	KM actions	Audience	Measure
Improve % of tenders won by 20% over next five financial years	Develop "tenders" area of intranet, including knowledge pack, precedents, or standard clauses, after action learning wiki (within 10 weeks) Organize and support face-to-face AAR meetings following successful and unsuccessful tenders Develop or improve thereafter (continuous)	Executive Board and Partnership Community of users	**Quantitative, leading (inputs)** Hits on "tenders" intranet pages and dwell times (monthly) Downloads of precedents or standard clauses (monthly) Numbers of contributions to the AAL wiki (monthly) Time spent by fee earners preparing tenders (using a specific time code) (monthly) Time spent by fee earners in developing "tenders" package (using a specific time code) (monthly) (KM staff time is considered a sunk cost) **Quantitative, lagging (downstream, result)** Number of tenders won and percentage (monthly) **Qualitative, leading** Informal feedback discussions with user groups (monthly) User group feedback survey and meeting to measure satisfaction with quality and ease of use (annually) Post-tender client feedback form (after each tender)

References

1. Kaplan, R. and Norton, D. 1992, 'The Balanced Scorecard – Measures That Drive Performance', *Harvard Business Review*, January/February, pp. 71–79
2. Kaplan, R. and Norton, D. 2001, 'Transforming the Balanced Scorecard from Performance Measurement to Strategic Management: Part 1', *Accounting Horizons*, Vol. 15 No. 1, March, pp. 87–104
3. Kaplan, R. and Norton, D. 2001, 'Transforming the Balanced Scorecard from Performance Measurement to Strategic Management: Part 1', *Accounting Horizons*, Vol. 15 No. 1, March, pp. 71
4. Rumizen, M. (2008). *The Complete Idiot's Guide to Knowledge Management*, p. 228
5. Although "data" is strictly a plural term, I use the more common singular.
6. Note the difference in meaning of "gaming" and "gamification". Gamification is the use of elements of game playing (psychology of engagement, competition, point scoring, badges, game levels) to drive behaviors in other fora, such as marketing, KM and other business systems. Gaming is the often-subconscious change in behavior when people aim to fulfil the measurement itself, rather than the objective behind the measurement. See page 11.
7. Neely, A., Adams, C., & Kennerley, M. (2002). The performance prism, the scorecard for measuring and managing business success. London: FT Prentice Hall, via Chaffey, D. and Wood, S. (2005). *Business Information Management: Improving Performance using Information Systems*, Financial Times Press, p. 529, via Russell, H. (2012). *Knowledge Management Handbook*, Law Society: London.

Chapter 2:
Are you your vendor's captive? How to optimize your research dollars

By Oz Benamram, Chief Knowledge Officer, White & Case LLP, and Kathy Skinner, Director of Research & Information Services, White & Case LLP

What do you do when one of your most longstanding and costly vendor relationships takes a dramatic turn for the worse? When your "preferred provider" no longer appears interested in offering their product to you at a price that reflects declining use and a growing number of alternatives in the market? When the relationship makes you feel like a hostage instead of a partner? That was our situation, and we are sharing our story in the hope that it will resonate with and help others.

It will come as no surprise to the law firm audience that the world of legal information has fundamentally changed in recent years. As the landscape of research tools continues to evolve in some exciting and useful ways, we need to continually reexamine past, well-reasoned choices and longstanding biases and make hard decisions about which resources stay and which ones go in our firms, driven by the ever-shifting tension between cost and benefit. Firms can no longer support expensive research resources that come with vendor-mandated requirements to purchase large sets of redundant content or enterprise-wide access that is neither needed nor desired. In addition, firms have strong incentives to free up budget for forward-looking tools with analytics and AI features that can anticipate future legal practice needs and are being developed and offered largely outside of the traditional research vendor realm.

These and other reasons compelled White & Case to forge a new and ongoing path toward optimizing our portfolio of research tools, driving toward a complement of unique research tools that meet practice needs, do not overlap significantly, and deliver appropriate value. This is our story and roadmap.

We wanted to:

- Give our lawyers all of the tools they need to practice;

- Stop charging our clients for database usage (they do not like paying for it); and
- Offer dedicated researchers for initial research to increase efficiency and improve quality.

If content can be seen as a continuum rather than a wholesale shift, we started to move along the continuum gradually, initially eliminating duplicative print and promoting and training on digital alternatives. Ultimately, we want to reach a point where we maintain an information ecosystem, with our users nimbly and comfortably adjusting to ongoing change and evolution into new products that deliver value in new ways.

Not about going sole provider

The world of legal information products is dominated by just a few suppliers. To appropriately evaluate and balance our resources, we knew that we needed to consider the role these major players have in our strategy. Achieving our long-term goals necessitated a strict and honest evaluation of our existing tools, especially those from our major players who reap the largest share of our budget and have the most overlapping content. In her post on *3 Geeks and a Law Blog* earlier this year, and Marcia Burris discussed why "Sole Provider Isn't Really a Thing".[1] Marcia suggests the view that we at White & Case share: the discussion should be around "legal research optimization" and "should include sub-points related to content (primary and secondary), efficiency of use and administration, attorney support, resource interrelatedness and content integration, cost, practice-specific needs, business needs, evolving technology, and client demands. Rather than allowing the status quo to set the tone of our discussions, let's ask what we should include as we build the law library of the future for our firms."

As we studied surveys and articles, spoke to many of our peers, and gained insights from our consultants, a number of things became evident:

- While reports ranged from 25 to 35 percent of AmLaw 200 firms currently stating they have a sole provider, firms are neutral on the selection of their supplier of choice; year-over-year growth among this group is small but persistent;
- Unsuccessful attempts to take this path appeared to be rooted primarily in moving too fast, motivated by solely cost-cutting

concerns rather than a broad view to change the firm's research and information paradigms (optimizing); and

- Success rarely accompanied a "keeping up with the Joneses" mentality. While the question "What are my peers doing?" was often asked, decision-making always focused on a firm's specific needs and, fundamentally, on whether the firm still receives good value for information the major players provide relative to the cost they demand.

After considering these factors, White & Case's specific needs, and diminished value from one of our largest supplier relationships (Vendor A), we determined that the price demanded was not worth the value received. When the vendor refused to negotiate with us, we decided that to advance on the content continuum, going to a sole provider was a reasonable and compelling option to pursue as a step toward meeting our goals.

Cost as a driver

For most firms, the aggregate cost of research and information products makes the top-five list in terms of overall expense. However, given the role these tools play in producing client work, practitioners typically prefer other austerity measures, rather than drastically reducing research tools. However, early in our analysis at White & Case, we identified an unusual factor. Because clients pushed back on our recovering costs for online legal resources, lawyers deliberately sought ways to do the same research at a lower cost to the client. In other words, they avoided and used only as the last resort the content providers to whom we paid the most. To test our theory – that lawyer resource selection was based more on cost than other preferences – we instituted a six-month trial period during which our lawyers could have, in addition to the current offerings, unlimited use of one supplier (Vendor B, a competitor of our historic preferred provider) at no cost to the clients. Within days of our announcement, we witnessed a reduction of over 65 percent in Vendor A usage. Additionally, we had anticipated that lawyers would return to the paid tools for periodic access to specific resources; instead, most lawyers remained satisfied within the free environment (see Figure 1).

Communication is key

Consistent communication is central to managing change. Like many knowledge management (KM) change initiatives, changing research

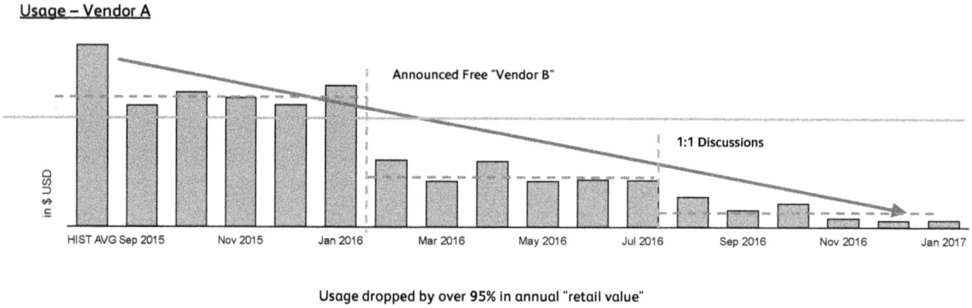

Figure 1: Effect of free service on usage of historically preferred service

information tools is highly sensitive as it has a personal impact on most users. Kris Martin (Senior Director for HBR Consulting who has worked with dozens of firms on similar initiatives) consulted for us on this project, designing and helping us execute a communication plan that ensured that we communicate appropriately with the various constituencies that would be affected.

Our process began in 2015 by communicating the vision to our administrative and legal leadership team. After securing the support of leadership, we kept them in the loop by establishing a regimen for communicating key updates. As we implemented each move along the continuum, our support from leadership was reaffirmed.

Data gathering and usage analysis also played a large role in this project. Obtaining accurate user information is a critical element to understanding needs and practices and recognizing potential pitfalls. Although an initiative as far-reaching as this does require an open survey, we followed this up with direct one-on-one conversations with users. Possible solutions were refined to address both macro and individual needs.

Finally, communicating clearly with our suppliers was crucial. At no point were we unclear about our long-term strategy. We found that some (though not all) suppliers, when given information and insight into our firm's direction, adapted their content, pricing, and support to align with our long-term goals. Those are the vendors with whom we have developed strong partnerships and made longer-term commitments. When we were unable to reach that level of understanding or alignment with our suppliers, we made the difficult decision to decrease or eliminate our usage of their product over time.

Where to begin

We started with two layers of assessment. First, we conducted a survey to determine feasibility. With this light-touch approach, we incorporated financial elements such as cost and cost recovery, quantitative usage elements identifying preferences and key content sets, and qualitative inputs both from user surveys and interviews with key constituents. These inputs allowed us to form our initial recommendations, spark dialogue with the leadership team, and obtain feedback from suppliers.

Next, we did a deep dive into our actual usage to fully vet the financial impact (risk and reward), communicate with and understand specific needs from our users, and work with our consultant and suppliers to align viable solutions to our users' needs. With this layer of assessment, we finalized our recommendation and received our leadership's approval.

Successful user dialog

To get quality user input, we used HBR's methodology for customizing interviews to each user by creating change personas. For instance, users deemed to be low-risk received a simple email questionnaire as a follow-up to the survey, while higher-risk users were called directly. Personas helped to identify whether that call should come from the library, leadership, or a senior member of the user's practice. Specific details of the user's content usage helped to inform the interviewer before calling.

Indeed, leveraging a customized version of HBR's SpendConnect (a business intelligence dashboard), allowed us to quickly understand individual usage at a glance, anticipate areas of concern, and be prepared with tailored solutions on the call (see Figure 2). This helped make each user feel heard and able to benefit from tailored solutions.

Our users confirmed the adage, "People don't fear change, they fear the unknown". Product familiarity was by far the greatest driver of usage. Sixty-five percent of survey respondents and over three-quarters of the people we interviewed cited familiarity as their top or only concern. Clearly, good training is important to managing change, but equally important is allowing time for people to adopt new behaviors and ditch long-held habits.

Engaging our users in direct conversation taught us about smaller operational or technical concerns that we could address and solve, strengthening our relationships with our users. This also provided us another opportunity to communicate our mission and goals for the project.

Figure 2: Usage analysis available through SpendConnect

Enhancing the toolkit

As observed above, one of our key goals was to ensure that users have the tools they need to be effective. As many of you likely have experienced, many powerful new products aimed at increasing the efficiency and effectiveness of our lawyers are on the market. Traditionally, our ability to offer these high-demand products was limited by budget. Once we released Vendor A and secured our long-term relationship with Vendor B, we could focus on enhancing our collection's value. Each law firm will find different value in the array of products out there. In our case, we added enterprise Bloomberg Law (our emerging "Vendor C"), enhancing access to practical guidance, news, analysis, data visualization tools, and market data, as well as primary and secondary law sources. We also added other innovative research and analytics tools, including CARA by CaseText, Ravel Law, and Lex Machina, all at a fraction of the cost of Vendor A, and at no cost to our clients. We knew, however, that fully leveraging these new search alternatives would require an expert team to guide and support our lawyers.

Increased user support

Our optimization project was an opportunity to not only introduce new research tools, but also to augment our research team and promote services we could not previously sustain, such as embedding researchers within practice groups. We are also using the optimization project to more actively market our library services, proactively monitor product usage, provide just-in-time training, and more fluidly navigate the wide array of product options to assure access to the best information at the lowest cost.

As Big Law increasingly finds itself competing with New Law, legal research is ripe for service transformation. The ABA survey and a study by Blue Hill Research both reveal that lawyers spend substantial time conducting legal research. While each firm draws the line between research and analysis at a different point, value comes from leveraging both efficient tools and experienced researchers.

Where do I start?

The content continuum presents a multi-year path that will differ for each firm but will represent a significant change for all. Assuring alignment with broader firm strategies, not to mention support for your overall research mission, is a critical first step. Once you have that support, define clear annual milestones with the understanding that some of these may take more than one year to accomplish. Leave time for your users to get comfortable with the alternatives.

Unless you have the rare privilege of being unconcerned with budget, as you identify new products and services that align with your mission, you will also need to make hard choices about your current collection. Before considering eliminating one of your providers, ask yourself the following:

- Are we getting the right value?
- Is usage low, particularly among lawyers and for secondary sources?
- Can content be found elsewhere?
- Do top users and practice groups support this decision?
- Will the firm support the decision?
- Will your other supplier support the transition?
- Are external pressures, such as cost recovery or alternative fee agreements, at play?

Finally, call us or reach out to colleagues and peers who have gone down similar paths to talk about their successes or pitfalls.

Our research tools and services optimization project was the right thing for our firm, despite the challenges and effort involved. We hope the analysis and discussion that we and many of our colleagues have undertaken will lead our vendors to work with us as partners, rather than insist on rigid models that are vestiges of a past that no longer supports our needs, and help us find the right solution for our firms as our needs evolve. Customers should never feel hostage to business and pricing models that are not in their and their clients' best interests, especially in times of rapid change and high pressure.

References

1. http://www.geeklawblog.com/2017/01/why-sole-provider-isnt-really-thing-and.html

Chapter 3:
Using KM to increase firm profitability and pricing predictability

By Jack Bostelman, president of KM/JD Consulting LLC, and Chris Boyd, senior director of professional services, Wilson Sonsini Goodrich & Rosati LLP

Introduction

Knowledge management (KM) can enable a firm to deliver greater value to clients by connecting each attorney to the expertise and experience of every other attorney in the firm. KM resources include work product (e.g., annotated forms, checklists and sample documents), matter profiles, expertise locators, and many others.

This chapter will explain how a firm can also use KM to increase firm profitability by setting forth a base-case profitability model and then showing through three case studies how the implementation of different KM resources can affect the model's variables in ways that increase overall profitability. A reader can adjust the model's inputs – attorney headcount, associate leverage, billing rates, etc. – to reflect her or his particular situation. The chapter will also show how effective KM can increase pricing predictability.

The first appendix to this chapter contains the full financial model calculations for each of the examples discussed in the chapter. A second appendix outlines practical techniques for implementing KM resources.

Case study one – Practice efficiency improvements

The first part of this discussion of practice efficiency improvements considers their effect on the firm as a whole (macro view). The second part considers their effect on an individual matter (micro view).

Macro view (entire firm)

The financial returns to a law firm from each type of KM project can be measured through the project's effect on the key financial drivers of profitability, which is the most essential financial metric for any business. The examples in this chapter illustrate the effects of three specific types of KM projects on these key financial drivers, and hence on law firm profitability.

Profitability is discussed as profits per partner, which allows comparisons across the different examples. "Partner" means "equity partner" unless otherwise stated. Definitions of the key financial drivers of profitability are in the sidebar. The full model calculations are included in Appendix A.

Assumptions used in the models

The examples in this chapter are based on the following assumptions:

- Firm size: 100 lawyers;
- Leverage: 50 partners/50 associates;
- Expense ratio: 50 percent;
- Billing rates and billable hours (utilization):
    - Partners $500/hour – 1,100 hours/year; and
    - Associates $250/hour – 1,400 hours/year.

Those assumptions result in the following revenues and profits:

- Total collected billings (revenues) = $45 million; and
- Profits per partner = $450,000.

In general, the greater the associate leverage or the higher the billing rates or annual billable hours, the greater will be the profits per partner improvements in the three examples. The size of the firm has relatively little effect on the results.

Example 1 – Practice efficiency improvements

The first example illustrates the effect of practice efficiency improvements on profitability. In this scenario, the firm seeks to reduce write-downs and write-offs by performing the same work in less time. The billable time saved would be spent working on new billable matters, in which case Utilization would not decline. If the program works:

- Realization Rate will increase.

  Because in this scenario efficiency savings go straight to the firm's bottom line, the benefit can be dramatic. If 5 percent of partner

> hours and 10 percent of associate hours are currently not collected because of write-downs and write-offs, and the program cuts those non-collected hours in half, profits per partner will increase by 8 percent. Even if the program cuts those non-collected hours by only 10 percent, profits per partner will still increase by 2 percent.
>
> If new billable work is not available, the decline in Utilization – in other words lawyers working fewer hours – will offset the Realization Rate improvement, resulting in no change in profits per partner. Lawyers will have more available time, however, to work on developing new business or improving their skills.

Of course, this example begs the question of what specific practice improvements are envisioned. Some examples are discussed later in this chapter. The point of this financial example is that an improvement in Realization Rate through efficiency gains has a powerful effect on profits per partner, and is an area in which it is worth focusing KM efforts.

It should also be noted that, whatever practice improvements are employed, some amount of billable time during the first year will need to be redirected to build the KM resources being used, and possibly some billable time will need to be redirected in future years to maintain those resources. That time investment will reduce the profitability improvements shown. If most of the investment occurs in the first year, however, the returns for *each* year in the future will be at or close to the return shown, with no further investment needed.

Micro view (individual matter)

Effective KM can not only increase the overall profitability of a firm, but also increase the profitability of specific matters. The clearest way to show this is with a fixed-fee matter, which is both topical and realistic given that the prevalence of these kinds of matters is increasing. For example, consider the following assumptions for a straightforward fixed-fee transaction:

- Fixed fee for services: $25,000;
- Average time recorded: 88 hours, comprised of:
  - Partner: 20 hours @ $500/hour = $10,000;
  - Associate: 48 hours @ $250/hour = $12,000; and
  - Paralegal: 20 hours @ $150/hour = $3,000.

Now assume the firm invests in KM resources that reduce the time required to conduct due diligence and draft deal documents by an average of five associate hours per transaction. These resources could include form documents, checklists, and perhaps even artificial intelligence tools. The firm could apply that saved time – five associate hours at $250 / hour, or $1,250 – in several ways: (a) retain it as per-matter profit, (b) pass it along to the client via a lower fixed fee, or (c) some combination of both. When multiplied by hundreds of matters (assuming that the matter type is relatively frequent), the aggregate savings to the firm, the client, or both can be substantial.

Two caveats should be noted in connection with this example:

- For the scenarios where the firm retains some or all of the savings, the per-matter profit to the firm will not increase by the full amount of the saved hours multiplied by the hourly billing rate. Rather, this profit will be discounted by both the percentage of saved hours that the firm can apply to other paying work as well as the realization rate on the re-used hours. For example, if 100 percent of the saved hours are applied to new work, and the realization rate on that work is 90 percent, then the additional profit to the firm is $1,125 and not $1,250.
- The total return to the firm of these KM investments must also be reduced by the cost of the investments, including the attorney time required to develop the resources, the licensing cost of any content or software involved in the resources, and so forth.

Drivers for professional services firms that use hourly billing

In professional services firms that bill by the hour, the following formula with five drivers explains profits per partner:

Profits per partner =

Realization rate (actual revenues ÷ standard rate revenues*) **x**

Average standard rate (standard rate revenues* ÷ # hours billed) **x**

Leverage (# timekeepers ÷ # partners) **x**

Margin (revenues - expenses, as a percent of revenues) **x**

Utilization (# hours billed ÷ # timekeepers)

This five driver model is most relevant to our discussion because, at least for now, hourly billing remains the predominant approach among Am67

Law 200 firms (in other words, the 200 largest US law firms by revenues, as reported annually by the *American Lawyer*). Timekeepers consist of partners, counsel, associates, paralegals, and certain other specialists who bill by the hour, with partners (equity and non-equity) and associates responsible for the great majority of time billed.

In business terms, these five drivers can be thought of as follows:

- **Realization rate** is the percentage of standard billing rates that is actually collected. It reflects agreed-upon discounts from standard rates, write-downs (fee reductions taken before sending the bill), and write-offs (fee reductions after sending the bill).
- **Average standard rate** represents the blended hourly rate for the firm that would have been realized if billed hours were collected at standard rates. Average standard rate times realization rate equals the firm's actual average hourly rate.

  [**Average realized rate**, which for brevity is used in the models in this chapter, is simply the product of realization rate and average standard rate.]
- **Leverage** is the ratio of fee-earners to equity owners – conceptually the associate/partner ratio. Mathematically, Leverage is 1 plus the associate/partner ratio.
- **Margin** is the traditional profit margin concept – the percentage of revenues that become profit after payment of related expenses.
- **Utilization** is also sometimes referred to as Productivity. It is the average number of hours billed by each timekeeper during the period being considered. For a firm that bills by the hour, the most productive timekeepers are those who work the most hours.

Success towards the KM goals of improved efficiency, improved quality, and reduced risk can be measured in terms of the five drivers. Improved efficiency could increase Realization Rate by reducing write-downs and write-offs or could increase Leverage. Improved quality could increase Realization Rate or the Average Standard Rate. Reduced risk could prevent a lower Realization Rate or Average Standard Rate, or could avoid expenses that reduce Margin.

*Standard rate revenues are the revenues that would have been earned if the hours of the various timekeepers had been billed at the firm's standard hourly rates.

Further explanation of efficiency and its benefits

Efficiency is producing what the client perceives as the same legal result in fewer hours or with lower-priced lawyers, such as:

- performing the same work more efficiently to reduce the cost to the firm;
- eliminating waste; or
- avoiding what is not needed or valued by the client.

Faster response time may also be a positive byproduct of improved efficiency, but is not the driving objective. Actions that may reduce cost or waste include:

- staffing with the lowest cost lawyers who are competent to perform the work;
- use of KM resources, templates or checklists; or
- legal process improvement.

Improved efficiency brings two important benefits: happier clients and happier lawyers. Clients are happier because they experience:

- lower legal fees for the same or even higher quality results;
- quicker turnaround; and
- less time managing outside counsel.

The firm's lawyers are happier because they experience:

- improved realization and profitability;
- better client relationships and referrals;
- efficient client teams who know the clients' industries; and
- more time for business development or a personal life.

Clearing up a financial misconception

A common misconception is that lawyers who bill by the hour have no economic incentive to become more productive or efficient. The examples discussed in this chapter demonstrate that assertion to be untrue. Example 1, showing the increase in profits per partner caused by reducing write-offs and write-downs, illustrates this point in a straightforward way.

Even where a firm has no write-offs or write-downs, as long as there is new work available to use up the lawyers' freed-up time, financial modeling shows that improved efficiency will not reduce profits per partner, which will remain unchanged, even as fees to clients for each matter *decline*. That is advantageous because it makes the firm more fee-competitive, enables the firm to deliver more value to clients, and increases the strength of the firm's client relationships.

Even where available new work is scarce for a firm, it is likely that other firms will be making the same kind of efficiency improvements, on the expectation that they can get new work through the lower fees resulting from efficiency. To remain competitive and avoid losing work, the firm without new work will still need to lower its fees. In the absence of efficiency improvements, the firm can lower its fees only through write-downs. As shown by Example 1, efficiency improvements will reduce those write-downs and increase the lawyer time available for seeking new business.

How KM can increase fee predictability

Clients and firms both want legal fees to be more predictable. Greater fee predictability helps clients better evaluate firms, budget for legal spending, and assess value delivered. Greater fee predictability also helps firms win and retain business, staff matters, and improve service delivery.

Effective KM can increase fee predictability in two ways. First, tracking matters and profiling them in detail, and connecting those profiles to legal fees, can help firms better predict the likely fees of any potential matter. Detailed information about past cases or deals helps a firm's pricing professionals build better budgeting and pricing models to apply to future matters. In addition, a firm's finance or KM team can provide attorneys seeking to estimate fees for a current matter with apples-to-apples fee data from similar past matters.

Secondly, KM and training resources can help a case, deal, or other matter team deliver legal services more consistently, which helps that team's actual fees come in as close as possible to the predicted fees. Regardless of whether a firm is delivering the matter on a billable-hour or fixed-fee basis, hitting the estimated or fixed number makes both the client and the firm happier. Combining the pre-work training on how to do a specific type of work with in-the-moment forms, checklists, and other resources is a particularly effective way to ensure that relatively frequent and straightforward legal work is performed both well and efficiently.

Examples of KM resources

There are many types of KM resources. A few of the more common ones are described below.

1. **Work product**. Model and precedent documents that lawyers consult for guidance, or use as starting points for drafting new deal or case documents. Work product typically comes in the format of a Microsoft Word document (for forms and other models) or scanned PDFs (for matter precedents). Some firms have automated model documents using document assembly software. Good models and precedents help lawyers draft new work product more efficiently with greater consistency and quality, thereby clients receive better work faster. Note that work product can be internal (such as briefs previously drafted by the firm) or external (such as other firms' responses to regulatory inquiries, or model forms from third-party subscription services such as Practical Law Company or Practising Law Institute). Similarly, work product can be made available to a practice group, an entire firm, the firm and select clients, or the firm and all clients.
2. **Matter experience databases**. Searchable descriptions and meta-data of deals, cases, and other matters, combined with key matter documents. Lawyers can search these profiles to find matters similar to ones they are working on to see how "market" terms are evolving, to get documents from past deals that may provide good starting points for research or drafting, to estimate fees for future matters, to find who in the firm has worked on similar issues, to put together a matter experience list for a new client pitch, and so forth. Matter experience databases can also be internal (such as homegrown deal databases) or external (such as searchable interfaces compiled by vendors that aggregate publicly-filed deal and case information).
3. **Expertise locators**. Resources that enable lawyers to find an expert who knows something or someone. The expertise can be general, for example Swedish mergers and acquisitions law, or specific, such as recent experience addressing a specific Securities and Exchange Commission comment in a recent initial public offering. As above, these resources can be internal (such as an expertise-focused search engine or a proprietary law firm or witness database) or external.
4. **Training**. Group training and individual mentoring that helps the firm's lawyers do their jobs well. This includes substantive training,

> such as the formal junior lawyer programs and "adult education" training given to senior associates and partners, and the informal training that occurs at practice group meetings. This formal substantive training can be internal or external. Training for KM purposes also includes formal and informal training about how to discover and use the firm's KM resources themselves. While many law firm KM leaders would not consider training to be part of KM, others would, and we have included it here to show the returns to initiatives that blend KM and training.

There are many other types of KM resources. These include holding effective practice group meetings, creating a culture of sharing information and ready collaboration, checklists describing steps to complete a matter or parts of a matter (aka playbooks), annotated checklists in lieu of standard forms, and specialized software such as products designed to summarize contract terms or analyze the range of variations of certain types of provisions across a collection of contracts of the same type.

While these kinds of KM resources are traditionally thought of as investments in the quality of work product and client service, they can and should also be used to increase firm profitability and pricing predictability. The next sections of this chapter will outline two more financial examples showing how investment in a KM initiative can increase firm profitability.

Second financial case study – shift work from partners to associates

The second financial case study involves a KM initiative with a more complicated effect on the key drivers of profitability.

By developing KM tools and rolling them out with targeted associate training, the firm seeks to shift some of its work from partners to associates, in effect moving the associates up the work food chain and providing more value to clients by delivering work of equivalent quality at a lower price. For example, a firm's patent litigation practice might spot an opportunity to take on more defense cases against non-practicing entities by delegating much of the work traditionally done by partners to associates. To do this, the firm invests in the development of pre-approved templates for standard case documents, checklists and other matter management tools to help keep the cases on track, and detailed training for associates on how to use them to achieve good results quickly for clients.

This initiative, if successful, will require hiring more associates to handle the greater workload. The goal is that partners use most of their new "free" time to take on new work on the same basis (in terms of the five profitability drivers) as existing work. Servicing that new work will also require hiring additional associates. Some of the partners' new "free" time will also need to be spent training associates, and some of the associates' time will need to be spent attending training. If this program works:

- Leverage will increase because of the additional associates;
- Average Standard Rate will decline because associates are billed at lower hourly rates than partners;
- Utilization will increase because there will be more associates (who generally work longer hours) in the mix; and
- Possibly, Realization Rate will increase because partners may be willing to bill and clients more fully to pay the lower fees resulting from a greater associate mix.

The goal is that the decreases in Average Standard Rate will be more than offset by improvements in the other drivers, resulting in higher profits per partner – notably, while also reducing the cost to clients of the work! Using the assumptions previously noted regarding partner/associate mix, billing and realization rates, margin and annual hours billed, *if*:

- Half the partners shift one billable hour per week to preparing the KM tools and conducting the training;
- All the associates shift one billable hour every other week to learning how to use the KM tools and attending training;
- The tools and training result in associates taking on 15 percent of partner work at the rate of 1.5 hours of associate time per partner hour assumed (on the theory that the associates, even with tools and training, cannot complete the work as fast as the partners);
- Saved partner time is devoted to new fee-paying work; and
- More associates are hired to help partners on the new work,

then profits per partner will *increase* 5.3 percent (even with no improvement in Realization Rate) and clients will see a 4.1 percent fee *reduction*.

Example 2 assumes more billable work is available. If it is not, profits per partner decline marginally, and partners have more time to work on developing new business – which, all else being equal, may be more likely to be obtained given the increased value the firm is delivering to its clients and their increased satisfaction level. This and other consequences of new work not being available have been discussed above under "Clearing up a financial misconception".

Third financial case study – more efficient partner pitch preparation

The third example illustrates another situation in which a KM initiative affects multiple financial drivers and has the net effect of increasing profits per partner.

Through improved data collection about matters, the firm seeks to save partner time in preparing and revising pitch materials, allowing the partners to apply that saved time to billable work. (Again, Example 3 assumes more billable work is available. If it is not, the project may improve the partners' quality of life but would not improve profits.) For example, the firm establishes a deal database for its transactional matters with sufficient detail to allow the marketing department to quickly and accurately show experience with specific kinds of transactions in specific industries, and a similar litigation case database containing experience with specific legal issues in specific jurisdictions (or even with specific judges). These databases are intended to eliminate the time spent by partners contacting their colleagues for this information.

If the program works:

- Utilization will increase because partners are billing more hours; and
- Average Standard Rate will increase slightly because of the greater number of partner hours in the mix.

Using the same law firm assumptions as the previous examples, if half the partners save two billable hours per week, profits per partner will *increase* about 6 percent (assuming no change in annual expenses).

Somewhat surprisingly, the cost of the new data collection system does not affect the outcome very much. For a 100-lawyer firm, a one-time $200,000 cost would reduce the profits per partner benefit by only 1 percent in the first year (to 5 percent), with no reduction in future years. Profit improvement is fairly linear to the time saved by partners. If half the partners save only one-quarter of a billable hour per week, profits per partner improve only 0.3 percent, which in practical terms is probably the break-even point for this initiative.

Investment of billable time to create the database will reduce the first-year benefit somewhat. Any ongoing billable time required to maintain the database in future years will also reduce the benefit a bit in those years. These time investments should be estimated and modeled before the initiative is undertaken. In addition, there may be other efficiency benefits of the initiative that should be modeled, such as using the database to more quickly identify similar matters for purposes of finding example documents.

Conclusion

This chapter has sought to demonstrate that changes to the way lawyers practice can have real financial benefits to both firms and clients. Any project can be analyzed under the law firm financial model. Of course, possible benefits used as model inputs are inherently judgment calls. One way to view the analysis of the model is as a way to discover the break-even point for benefits. After determining the assumptions that lead to the break-even point, ask yourself and your colleagues whether they believe that level of benefit is achievable. If there is reasonable confidence the break-even level will be achieved, then it makes sense to proceed with the initiative.

Appendix A – The three financial models

Base Case – Financial model for hourly billing

	Average annual billable hours	Average annual written-off hours	Average annual non-billable admin hours
Partners	1,100	58	100
Associates	1,400	156	50

Billing rate	# in firm
$500	50
$250	50
Total lawyers	100

Annual expenses = $22,500,000

Average realized rate = total annual billings ÷ # hrs billed

Total billings = (1,100*$500*50) + (1,400*$250*50) =	$	45,000,000.00
# hrs billed = (1,100*50) + (1,400*50) =		125,000
ARR =	$	360.00

Leverage = # lawyers ÷ # partners

Leverage = (50 + 50) ÷ 50 = 2.00

Margin = (total annual billings - expenses) ÷ total annual billings

Margin = ($45,000,000 - $22,500,000) ÷ $45,000,000 = 50 %

Utilization = total annual hours billed ÷ # lawyers

Utilization = (1,100*50 + 1,400*50) ÷ (50+50) = 1,250

Profit Per Partner = ARR * Leverage * Margin * Utilization = $ 450,000.00

Example 1 – Practice efficiency improvements

5 percent of partner hours and 10 percent of associate hours are written off before or after the bill is sent, due to inefficiency or client fee sensitivities.

Through practice improvements, the lawyers become efficient enough that matters are completed in fewer hours.
As a result, written off hours are reduced 50 percent, with those saved hours being billed and collected on other new work.
For simplicity, the model treats all write-offs as soft, with 100 percentage of billings being collected.

	Average annual billable hours	Average annual written-off hours	Average annual non-billable admin hours	Billing rate	# in firm
Partners	1,129	29	100	$500	50
Associates	1,478	78	50	$250	50
				Total lawyers	100

Annual expenses = $22,500,000

			Base Case
Average realized rate = total annual billings ÷ # hrs billed			
Total billings = (1,129*$500*50) + (1,478*$250*50) =		$ 46,700,000.00	$ 45,000,000.00
# hrs billed = (1,129*50) + (1,478*50) =		130,350	125,000
ARR =		$ 358.27	$ 360.00
Leverage = # lawyers ÷ # partners			
Leverage =	(50 + 50) ÷ 50 =	2.00	2.00
Margin = (total annual billings - expenses) ÷ total annual billings			
Margin =	($46,700,000 - $22,500,000) ÷ $46,700,000 =	52 %	50 %
Utilization = total annual hours billed ÷ # lawyers			
Utilization =	(1,129*50 + 1,478*50) ÷ (50+50) =	1,304	1,250
Profit Per Partner = ARR * Leverage * Margin * Utilization =		$ 484,000.00	$ 450,000.00

Result: Profits per partner improve by $34,000 (8 %), or a total of $1,700,000 per year.

Example 2 – Shift work from partners to associates

Half the partners shift this many hours per week (percentage of average billable time) to training & forms:	1.00 (2.3 %)
All the associates shift this many hours per week (percentage of average billable time) to attending training:	0.50 (1.8 %)
As a result, additional associates take on this percentage of partner billable time, at the rate of 1.5 associate hours per partner hour assumed and with no added partner hours for supervision:	15 %

Partners devote their spare billable time (difference of above items) to new work, using additional associates at the same leverage.

Increase in number of associates is 18 (8.8 to handle former partner work and 8.7 for new work, rounded up).

Expenses increase at 50 percent of per associate billing rate to reflect new associate salaries and overhead.

	Average annual billable hours	Average annual written-off hours	Average annual non-billable admin hours	Billing rate	# in firm
Partners	1,075	57	125	$500	50
Associates	1,375	153	75	$250	68
				Total lawyers	118

Annual expenses = $26,550,000

			Billings for old work:
Average realized rate = total annual billings ÷ # hrs billed			
Total billings = (1,075*$500*50) + (1,375*$250*68) =		$ 50,250,000.00	$ 43,140,625.00
# hrs billed = (1,075*50) + (1,375*68) =		147,250	**Base Case**
ARR =		$ 341.26	$ 360.00
Leverage = # lawyers ÷ # partners			
Leverage =	(68 + 50) ÷ 50 =	2.36	2.00
Margin = (total annual billings - expenses) ÷ total annual billings			
Margin =	($50,250,000 - $26,550,000) ÷ $50,250,000 =	47 %	50 %
Utilization = total annual hours billed ÷ # lawyers			
Utilization =	(1,075*50 + 1,375*68) ÷ (50+68) =	1,248	1,250
Profit Per Partner = ARR * Leverage * Margin * Utilization =		$ 474,000.00	$ 450,000.00

Result: Profits per partner improve by $24,000 (5.3 %), or a total of $1,200,000 per year.
Note that ARR and margin decline slightly.
Billings to clients for old work actually decline 4.1 %.

Example 3 – More efficient partner pitch preparation

Additional annual partner billable hours per partner: 50
No increase in total annual expenses.

	Average annual billable hours	Average annual written-off hours	Average annual non-billable admin hours	Billing rate	# in firm
Partners	1,150	61	50	$500	50
Associates	1,400	156	50	$250	50
				Total lawyers	100

Annual expenses = $22,500,000

			Base Case
Average realized rate = total annual billings ÷ # hrs billed			
Total billings = (1,150*$500*50) + (1,400*$250*50) =		$ 46,250,000.00	$ 45,000,000.00
# hrs billed = (1,150*50) + (1,400*50) =		127,500	125,000
ARR =		$ 362.75	$ 360.00
Leverage = # lawyers ÷ # partners			
Leverage =	(50 + 50) ÷ 50 =	2.00	2.00
Margin = (total annual billings - expenses) ÷ total annual billings			
Margin =	($46,250,000 - $22,500,000) ÷ $46,250,000 =	51 %	50 %
Utilization = total annual hours billed ÷ # lawyers			
Utilization =	(1,150*50 + 1,400*50) ÷ (50+50) =	1,275	1,250
Profit Per Partner = ARR * Leverage * Margin * Utilization =		$ 475,000.00	$ 450,000.00

Result: Profits per partner improve by $25,000 (6 %), or a total of $1,250,000 per year.

Appendix B – How to start/restart a KM practice efficiency program

Select a pilot practice group

A firm that wishes to start a KM practice efficiency program, or reinvigorate its existing efforts, should pilot its effort in a single practice group. Concentrating its efforts in one group will allow greater progress to be made, enabling the firm to demonstrate the benefits of the effort to other practice groups.

It is important that the candidate practice group be one whose leaders want to improve efficiency, even if they are unsure how to accomplish that. The group should also have enough visibility within the firm, by virtue of size or reputation, that its successes will be noticed by other groups.

Although each group's particular KM needs will differ, the pilot group's success will nevertheless inspire others to try, because many of the same KM concepts will work. For example, a checklist can benefit any practice group, even though the content of the checklist will be specific to a particular group.

Hold a meeting of the group

After the pilot group is identified, a kick-off meeting of the group should be held for the purpose of brainstorming KM ideas. The lawyers should be asked to think broadly. For example, they could be asked, "What changes would make your life easier as a practicing lawyer?"

In addition to gathering ideas from those who know what can really make a difference, the meeting serves the second important purpose of gaining buy-in from the group's lawyers because they "own" the ideas. The meeting should include one to two dozen lawyers, reflecting a cross-section of seniority levels from junior associate to senior partner and office locations. As many lateral lawyers as possible should be invited as well. They bring a helpful perspective because they can describe KM initiatives that have worked at their prior firms.

The meeting can be run by a partner of the firm or by an outside facilitator. The meeting leader should keep a list of all the suggestions. Even with a broad question such as the one suggested above, almost all the ideas will likely fall in the KM area.

Prioritize the KM projects

For the same reason the firm should focus its initial efforts in a single practice group, the practice group should focus its initial efforts on a limited number of initiatives. It is likely the ideas from the meeting will exceed the group's capacity to implement them. How, then, should the group's leader decide which opportunities to pursue and which to set aside, at least for the moment?

One useful prioritization method was set forth by Oz Benamram and Sally Gonzalez in a 2011 article.[2] The practice group, assisted by the KM team, should map potential KM projects on a two-by-two matrix, with one axis being ease of implementation and the other being value to the business, as illustrated below:

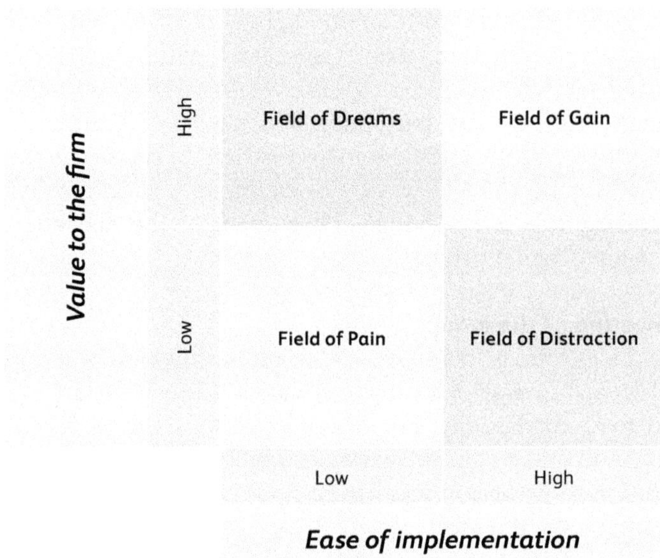

One way to accomplish that is for the practice group to assign a 1–5 rating to value (5 being highest) and ease of implementation (5 being easiest), then rank projects based on the sum of the two ratings. Values can be assigned in a variety of ways, from informally via show of hands at a meeting to more formally via detailed analyses and cost-benefit calculations. Assessing ease of implementation should take into account factors such as:

- Management and practice group support – the greater support is, the easier implementation will be;
- Number of lawyers who must cooperate – the lower the number, the easier implementation will be;

- Process feasibility – the fewer process changes required, the easier implementation will be;
- Technical feasibility – the less complex or dedicated technology required, the easier implementation will be; and
- Size of investment required for both development and maintenance – the lower the investment, the easier implementation will be.

For example, checklists are typically on the easier end of the spectrum, because they can be created by a few lawyers for the benefit of many, and at least at the basic level do not require dedicated technology. Assessing value to the business should take into account factors such as:

- The potential financial returns from the project, as discussed in this chapter;
- The potential non-financial returns from the project, including enhancing reputation and brand (or avoiding reputational harm), improving client satisfaction and improving lawyer morale and retention; and
- The number of people likely to use the resource to be developed, in other words, the target user group multiplied by the likely adoption rate. One way to assess this factor is to seek input at a meeting of 10–20 lawyers representing a cross-section of the affected practice group(s). This approach also aids acceptance of the project by the group because they are more likely to buy in to its rationale and potential benefits.

Once the KM projects are mapped onto the matrix, the team should go for the quick wins in the Field of Gain, steadily chip away at the Field of Dreams, and avoid the Fields of Pain and Distraction.

Implement the projects

Timing and accountability

Successful execution of top-priority projects depends on effective application of traditional accountability and project management techniques. First, the practice group should assign each project to a small team and staff it like a matter. A particularly notable way to instill accountability is to make the assignments at a practice group meeting, so that the attorneys' peers see who is on which projects.

Second, the group's leader(s) should set deadlines for all projects. The ideal scope is one achievable in six months – long enough to demonstrate clear accomplishments, yet short enough to maintain the momentum of the initiative and harness lawyers' natural tendencies for urgency. A three-month check-in at project midpoint can be a useful way to provide guidance and oversight along with any necessary course corrections and resource re-assignments.

Finally, to keep each project team focused, the practice group leader(s) should require the teams to provide weekly status reports that are circulated to the entire group. This both provides peer pressure and instills healthy and productive competition among the project teams.

Other implementation considerations

It is very likely that some of the group's KM projects will involve creation of materials to which lawyers in the group will need ready access on an ongoing basis – for example, checklists or a spreadsheet containing a master matter list with profile data. As part of the overall KM pilot initiative, the group should establish a way for group members to access these materials. An ideal location would be the group's intranet site. A byproduct of using the intranet is that it may be revitalized by having this fresh content. A shared drive or folder in the document management system could also be used, although those are typically not as user-friendly as an intranet site.

In order to reinforce that the firm values the KM initiatives of the practice group, and to align the incentives with that objective, billable hours credit (up to a reasonable cap) should be given for that work, if at all possible.

As a further technique to keep the group's practitioners focused on making progress on the KM initiative, the firm's leaders should demonstrate their support, such as by attending some of the practice group's meetings where progress on the KM initiative is being presented. Knowing the firm's managing partner will attend the meeting should further motivate lawyers to have something to present and should improve attendance by the rest of the group.

Conclusion

Implementation is important. That's where many projects fail. Start small – with a single practice group. Leadership of that group must be seen to be actively involved. Prioritize projects according to high value and low difficulty. Gain commitment from the practice group members and employ accountability techniques, such as those described above.

It is highly desirable to create success metrics for each project. The base level should be established before starting. Devising a way to measure the relevant factors and taking measurements could take some time and may delay the start of the project, but is the only way to be able to measure comprehensively the benefits of the project. When the project is complete, measure the factors again. While the measurement process itself may involve judgments and estimates, it can nevertheless be valuable in assisting the group in deciding what works and what does not as it decides how to allocate scarce practitioner resources to KM projects.

Finally, apply successes to other practice groups.

References

1. See, e.g. Boyd, C., 'Case Study: Using Document Assembly Tools to Improve Services to Start-Ups,' Legal Tech Newsletter (Law Journal Newsletters), October 2010, available at: www.wsgr.com/publications/PDFSearch/boyd1010.pdf.
2. Oz Benamram and Sally Gonzalez, "Forming a KM Strategy for Your Firm," *Knowledge Management White Paper* (International Legal Technology Association June 2011), available at http://www.iltanet.org/MainMenuCategory/Publications/WhitePapersandSurveys/Knowledge-Management_1.html.

Chapter 4:
Our "small" project with a big impact: Littler's Knowledge Desk, a case study

By Cynthia L. Brown, Director Research Services, Littler Mendelson P.C.

How do you fix something that no one thinks is broken? About four years ago, my boss talked about creating a help desk – a concierge for our attorneys, a place where attorneys could ask questions and be directed to the best resource. I didn't get it. Wasn't this just a new name for our Library Reference Desk?

Our library had a well-established and respected reputation within Littler. Our Knowledge Management (KM) attorneys' reputation was unprecedented. Attorneys asked us questions and received answers, so what needed to change? My boss already knew that any business looking to succeed must seek opportunities to change, innovate and evolve. Innovation need not come in the form of expensive new tools or sweeping, firmwide changes. Small changes can have a big impact.

Law firms often roll out multiple search engines, databases and portals to provide information to their lawyers, and are then surprised when lawyers don't use them. The belief is that lawyers don't use these tools because they are not tech-savvy. In reality, it's because there are too many options, and it can be difficult to figure out which tool to use and when.

Introducing Littler's Knowledge Desk

Littler's library, a division of the greater KM department, bridges information needs and answers through its one-stop-shop for all KM and library research inquiries and needs via the Knowledge Desk. The Knowledge Desk is available to all Littler attorneys and staff for any legal research, traditional library resources, KM requests or questions concerning our legal training group, Littler Learning Group (LLG). Via the Knowledge Desk, attorneys are connected to subject matter experts, a vast collection of databases, print materials, practice groups, internal work product, and proprietary data collections, through which our team can search efficiently to locate exact information. We had distinct goals when creating the Knowledge Desk:

1. Centralize the gathering of attorneys' questions;
2. Use library, KM, and LLG more efficiently;
3. Create time for higher level projects and innovation; and
4. Better serve our attorneys.

Our first step was to determine what types of questions were separately coming to the library, KM and LLG, and who was answering these questions. We reverse-engineered the services we were providing to our attorneys and staff. The team reviewed years of emails, and sifted through mountains of data collected in our ticket-tracking system. We discovered that questions were being sent to KM that should have been sent to the library, and high-level KM attorneys were gathering documents that could have been provided by a library assistant. We were doing the wrong work with the wrong people.

After our fact-finding, we mapped out types of requests, reviewed inquiries as they came in and then used data to shape our new policies and response protocols. We determined that all questions would be sent to one centralized email #KnowledgeDesk. The library created three teams to specialize in various types of tickets, and a system was created to elevate tickets to KM attorneys, LLG attorneys and KM management as needed. We spent significant time training the library staff to recognize KM questions and how to respond to those questions. During the pilot phase, KM attorneys were assigned to work in tandem with Librarians as we transferred work. Law firm librarians are perfectly suited to liaise between attorneys and a legal KM department, and our training and mentoring efforts served to enhance our librarians' abilities. The training and pilot phase were critical to our success. We understood that every question received had to provide outstanding responses to ensure total firmwide adoption of our new plan. We spent several months running the Knowledge Desk with oversight by our KM attorneys and LLG teams, and in the end the training from KM and LLG merged with the expertise of our library team to create an increased level of service.

Through the pilot phase we also dedicated time to cross training and thorough documentation of procedures. This not only brought the entire team up to speed quickly and accurately, but now running at full capacity this depth allows the Knowledge Desk to handle smoothly the inevitable ebb and flow of request levels. Our attorneys receive the same quality service whether it is a slow summer week with 400 requests, or the fall rush with requests surging to nearly 600 in a week.

Once we knew how we wanted the Knowledge Desk to run, and we completed a successful pilot, it was time to determine how we would announce our new tool to the firm. Collaborating with our marketing team, we developed a detailed campaign. We knew it had to be more than one email announcement; it had to feel different because it *was* different.

The announcement had to make a splash. A team, assembled from the library, KM, and marketing, worked together on a multilevel campaign for the launch. Our Managing Directors sent out a firmwide announcement that included an animated video explaining the Knowledge Desk. We put together an animation to explain the Desk, and why attorneys and other firm employees would want to use it. We also sent each attorney, paralegal and secretary a ceramic coaster with our new logo and tag line. We wanted the Knowledge Desk to be at the forefront of their minds. Every time they picked up their coffee mug, they would see: *#KnowledgeDesk: Your Answer is Here.*

After the initial launch, our job was not done. Emails sent to the old reference desk or KM group were redirected to #KnowledgeDesk. Direct calls to a KM attorney or our Management team were met with reminders that the Knowledge Desk would have the best answer. We continued our guerilla marketing efforts, to preach about the Knowledge Desk at every opportunity, and we continue to utilize the best marketing tool there is: exceptional service.

The Knowledge Desk strives to answer every question posed, even the seemingly odd questions such as those regarding exchanging money overseas, what rental car company to use, flight information from Los Angeles International Airport to Omaha, Nebraska, or how to order new business cards. We hold true to our tagline: *your answer is here.*

A logical offshoot of our online concierge was to find a way to help our attorneys help themselves (when possible). After the Knowledge Desk was firmly established, we created a portal for our information that allows attorneys to access its power conveniently. This portal is a part of the internal "Littler Apps" and is available to everyone at the firm. Several years ago, I attended a conference where a shareholder said, "I want a research librarian on call 24 hours a day. I want you to know what I need and be there to answer the phone when I need it." This is obviously neither practical nor sustainable, but the Knowledge Desk coupled with the portal comes closer to answering this shareholder's request than any other system I have seen.

Via the Knowledge Desk on LittlerApps, attorneys can explore the vast catalog of Littler's firmwide resources and get hold of documents or information they need at any time. The portal also holds research materials for frequent specialty research, such as legislative history, class action data, verdicts and settlements, and litigation profiles.

A comment we hear a lot is: "Well, I don't know if the Knowledge Desk can do [this] or not." The Knowledge Desk page creates live links to help with common requests. An attorney sees the request he/she needs, clicks on the button and it generates an email to the Knowledge Desk with prepopulated questions for the applicable information.

We also use the Knowledge Desk portal as a place to advertise and market our services. An attorney may come to the page for self-service, but end up learning about alert services, legislative tracking, or a new KM product.

The Knowledge Desk self-serve portal contains many of our KM products and tools, such as links to the Littler Employer Library, our employee handbook materials, a legislation resource page, current issues and archives of the Daily News, and other subject area news digests.

The portal also contains a tab for all library resources training. Materials are provided in several formats to fit differing needs. Training guides, demo videos and best practice tips are maintained and provided by the library team.

A year later, #KnowledgeDesk averages over 2,000 requests per month and has handled more attorney requests in the first nine months of 2017 than in all of 2016. We are on track to respond to over 26,000 requests by year-end – a 35% increase year-over-year. In the past 20 months, the number of "All Attorney" emails requesting basic or general information have dropped by over 50%, allowing our attorneys to spend time practicing law rather than digging through emails. #KnowledgeDesk continues to streamline workflow as the single point of contact for the Knowledge Management Attorneys, Research Librarians, and Littler Learning Group Trainers.

After this initial success, we will continue to work to improve and innovate delivering knowledge resources to our firm. We are now focusing on scaling the Knowledge Desk with smarter technology, automating processes as applicable and continuing to elevate each team member to continually improve the level and depth of service we can provide with minimal additional capital investment.

Our initial goals for the Knowledge Desk have been met:

1. Attorneys and staff no longer wonder who they should ask for help. Our triage system allows us to tap into institutional knowledge to direct inquiries to subject matter experts, practice groups, and department contacts. And our library provides content, internal and external, to our attorneys in the most efficient manner possible;
2. Our library team is better organized and all team members have new opportunities to work on a wider range of requests and elevated projects. Our KM and LLG attorneys have more time to work on the specialized projects they are uniquely qualified to lead, and;
3. Our efficiency has allowed us to focus on and continue to innovate.

As one of our shareholders has said: "The Knowledge Desk is the best thing Littler has ever done."

Chapter 5:
Library and knowledge management – a good fit

By Mark Gediman, director of research services, Best Best and Krieger LLP

One morning, in the not too distant past, I received an email from a partner with a question: Could the Library help him to create a specialized repository for specific documents from a select group of clients that would be easy to access? This is the very definition of knowledge management: making the information the individual needs to access available in the most intuitive way possible. I'll talk about the steps involved in making this happen a bit further into the chapter.

Law firm knowledge management usually encompasses information contained in the following areas:

- Document management systems;
- Records management systems;
- Legal research;
- Training and professional development;
- Litigation support including eDiscovery processes and procedures;
- Client-facing products; and
- Matter budgeting and alternative fee arrangements.

Document management systems

First, the information contained in the documents and records management systems are commonly referred to as the firm's "work product". Let's focus first on the document management system, commonly referred to as the DMS. The majority of these documents are produced as a result of, or related to, specific client projects and matters. As a result, these documents usually count in the millions and may date back to the early days of these systems, stretching back 20 years or more. This makes determining and compiling the best documents based on different needs difficult. It isn't very efficient to have attorneys spend hours, if not days or weeks, reviewing documents to create topical document repositories. This is an area where the librarian's skills in search and taxonomy can be very valuable.

Although you may be familiar with the term "Taxonomy," it may be useful to review a quick definition. *Merriam-Webster* defines the term as:

> *"classification; especially: orderly classification of plants and animals according to their presumed natural relationships."*
> Source: taxonomy. 2017. In Merriam-Webster.com. Retrieved November 30, 2011, from https://www.merriam-webster.com/dictionary/taxonomy

In a library, this term is typically used to identify a method of organizing information using short descriptive terms or codes. These taxonomies can be applied using terms from various sources. One commonly used taxonomy system is the Library of Congress Subject Headings (http://id.loc.gov/authorities/subjects.html). This system has existed since 1898 and, through many updates, remains an excellent source of classification of many types of information. However, it does have some drawbacks when attempting to apply it to information in a law firm context. For example, the term "civil discovery" is not included in this list. Also missing are "amicus," "wage and hour" and "mandamus".

Other taxonomy tools exist that have more relevance to the legal field. These tools include treatise table of contents, tagging, searchable document annotations and standardized headnotes. An excellent example of a headnote classification resource is *West's Analysis of American Law*, 2016 edition (Thomson Reuters). As described by the publisher:

> West's Analysis of American Law *is a complete guide to the West Key Number System, which organizes American case law into more than 400 main topics and over 100,000 individual lines.*

The key number system will provide standard terms for just about any topic covered in a law firm. This will provide a consistent structure and confidence that the terms will be widely recognized by the legal staff. If you have the companion West KM product, an integrated search tool automatically applies the key number to internal documents.

Tagging and annotating documents are features offered by some search engines, such as Lexis Search Advantage. This allows the flexibility of including topical terms, such as those taken from the table of contents of a specific practice's basic treatises and organizing the documents into a structure similar to that laid out in that table of contents. Using the table of contents to create a document tagging system allows for a structure tailored to the specific needs of the firm using terms from a resource they use regularly. For example, *California Tort Guide* (2017, CEB) includes a section on Premises Liability. In this section, the main headings are listed as follows:

1. Ordinary Care Standard (*Rowland v Christian*) 10.3;
2. Effect of Visitor's Status 10.4;
3. Owner's Conduct; Active Operations 10.5; and
4. Owner's Liability for Others' Conduct.

This system gives clear and concise terminology as well as a method for organizing the file structure of the best practice database for this specialized area of law.

The challenge of determining best practice documents without involving the attorneys in the early stages can be daunting. This is especially true because the process of determining a best practice document can be extremely subjective. One attorney's favorite document may not be considered to be all that great by another. The other problem is the issue of having the attorneys invest their valuable time in this potentially tedious, non-billable activity. This can make implementing a knowledge management system for these types of documents challenging to say the least.

One possible solution to this problem is to look at document activity counts. Most search engines for document management systems include the ability to view the activity or views received for each document in the system. A reasonable assumption, at least for the initial filtering stages, is that the documents with the highest number of views are perceived as best practice documents. Using this data point can significantly reduce the number of documents that would need to be reviewed for inclusion in the best practice collection. Quantifying what can be a subjective process is another advantage of this process.

Records management systems

Records management systems are not much different than document management systems. In fact, some classify document management systems as a type of records management system. However, the term "records management system" usually refers to the system used to track the hard copy client files of the firm. The knowledge management aspect of this is again the ability to find what the legal staff needs in a quick and intuitive manner. The librarian's unique knowledge of search techniques and how the attorneys work can make a difference in creating a useful system. The basics seem simple: type a client-matter number and view the records for the desired file. And it can be simple. In order to accomplish this simplicity, it is necessary to look at how results of this research are displayed. Providing too much information, such as listing out subfolders by default instead of providing a clear view with the option to drill deeper into the file structure will unnecessarily complicate the ability to find the needed file. Less is the goal here, without omitting important pieces of information such as retention dates and privacy restrictions.

Legal research

Legal research is one of the lesser known aspects of knowledge management. Hundreds of searches are run each month by library staff, attorneys, and paralegals. The details of these searches, including search techniques, lessons learned while conducting the research, and the resources found during the research are important information to not only the research professional but for the firm as well.

A common tool used to capture information on search techniques and lessons learned is a knowledge base. A knowledge base is organized along the lines of a traditional database and can be linked to the record of the original request in a library team management system such as Reference Tracker (eos), Quest, Quatrove, or Sydney Plus to retain information related to specific research requests. These databases can be purchased as an add-on component for the library management systems referenced above or created using the firm's document management system with an excel spreadsheet to record the original requests. Librarians can use this system to record their research methodology for difficult research projects and share knowledge with others to provide a guide for this type of research project.

Research projects often find items that can have value to others in the firm aside from the individual(s) that originated the project. The type of items with value beyond the initial research project include but are not limited to maps, government reports and studies. The goal is to make them accessible to anyone at any time who finds they need to review them during the course of their research. Here are a couple of simple cost-effective solutions:

1. In the document management system, create a client matter number specifically to house these documents. Then create topical subfolders and organize the documents accordingly; and
2. Add these items to the catalog in your Library Management System and organize the information along the same lines as other library materials.

Training and professional development

Training and professional development materials are typically items that are overlooked when examining the scope of the knowledge management system. These items are usually compartmentalized by department and are not organized topically. Rather, the default organizational scheme is usually based on the CLE requirement met, practice group who requested the professional development resource, or the type of administrative skill being taught. However, these items lend themselves very nicely to the taxonomy structures discussed above. A program purchased for the Real Estate Practice Group can be classified according to Premises Liability instead of being grouped together with programs on Sales Contracts and Deed of Trusts. Similarly, administrative training programs on creating a Table of Authorities can be tagged as a pleading or litigation process instead of being grouped with all of the training programs related to Microsoft Word.

Litigation support and eDiscovery databases

Litigation support and eDiscovery databases are often separate from the firm's document management systems and don't often receive the same attention as the more mainstream document repositories when it comes to applying the firm-wide organizational structure. There may be some disagreement about whether or not these should even be considered. These databases are intended to manage large amounts of documents specific to a particular case so the organization of the documents is often dictated by the litigation. However, applying the firm's taxonomy to these documents can give the reviewing attorneys and paralegals a familiar basis and mechanism for researching documents in the databases that may aid the process of finding relevant documents.

Client-facing products

Many firms have set up extranets or accessible external websites that allow the attorneys to collaborate and share documents with the clients directly. Just as the internal repositories mentioned above, these websites are also subject to becoming unwieldy over time. This can create frustration on the part of both the client and the attorney. Organizing the documents using a taxonomy common to both parties can make the sharing of information more intuitive and less frustrating. The folder structure and language will necessarily differ from what is used within the firm because the firm's filing methodology may not be intuitively understood by the client due to their different frame of reference. This should be taken into consideration when creating a structure for the extranet.

Matter budgeting and alternative fee arrangements

Matter budgeting and alternative fee arrangements are based on the idea that the firm can streamline their handling of specific matter types to limit client costs while still showing a profit. A good knowledge management system makes it easier to leverage prior work products and experiences to efficiently perform the requested task. This removes the necessity for the attorney to "reinvent the wheel" each time this task is performed.

Now for the request I mentioned at the start of this chapter: Could the Library create a specialized repository for specific documents from a select group of clients that would be easy to access?

To me, the most important part of this request is the very last phrase: "easy to access".

Below is my step-by-step process for responding to this request.

Full disclosure: This process is using iManage and Lexis Search Advantage (LSA). Your experience may vary based on the resources in your firm.

- Create a specific client matter worksite in the document management system to house the documents. NOTE: Keep the folder structure minimal. I only use the document folder. It makes it easier to populate the database later on.
- The separate client matter worksite creates a location that is separate from the document management system. This location also makes it easier to create an intuitive retrieval process for these documents. More on this below.
- Search on the specific documents and rank by activity count.
- As mentioned above, this is one way to determine popularity and usefulness.
- Make a list of the documents with the larger counts.

- These will be the documents that will be part of the Best Practices file.
- Copy these documents into the Documents folder in the worksite.
- Run different searches and save the URL for each one.

NOTE: Limit each search with the following criteria:

- The specific client matter number for the worksite.
- Use the specific document type.
- Any unique terminology.

LSA creates a fixed URL for each search session. It will automatically update the search with any documents that are added to the worksite each time the link is clicked.

- Add the URLs as links to the practice group.

The solution is just one of many ways that these can be set up. For instance, these documents could be tagged with standard terms that will allow them to be easily included in other searches run in the document management system. The idea was that every step would result in a system that was simple to update and simple to use. The less time spent searching for specific types of documents results in a more efficient process and less frustration by the attorneys.

Conclusion

One question I often get asked is should librarians be involved in knowledge management? My answer? Duh! Librarians have the skills and knowledge necessary to make any knowledge management program a success. The primary function of any librarian is to maintain and organize knowledge in a way that preserves it while simultaneously making it accessible. Librarians know the culture of the firm and have the frame of reference to tailor the knowledge retrieval process to the specific needs of the firm. The research skills of the librarian are essential in understanding how to organize the information so it can be found easily by non-library staff. This chapter has shown how the unique ability of librarians to organize information and understand how the end user looks for that information can make a knowledge management program successful.

Chapter 6:
Case study – Bringing lawyers out of their silos: promoting smart collaboration at Wolf Theiss

By Andrea Miskolczi, chief business development and marketing officer, Wolf Theiss

"I went to law school so that I could tackle sophisticated legal issues. If I wanted to manage teams, I would have gotten an MBA." Apparently, this is what a lawyer in a US firm said in Heidi Gardner's research about smart collaboration. Heidi Gardner, PhD, is a Distinguished Fellow in the Center on the Legal Profession at Harvard Law School, who focuses on leadership and collaboration in professional service firms.

The quotation perfectly illustrates the problem that large law firms often have: highly specialized lawyers prefer to work in their field (in their silos?) and perceive the collaboration process as inefficient and uncomfortable. This perceived inefficiency is one of the many barriers to collaboration – barriers that make it difficult for specialized lawyers to address their clients' highly complex problems.

Collaboration is a proven way to improve business results. As Dr. Gardner's research shows, smart collaboration supports higher levels of client satisfaction, higher levels of employee satisfaction, as well as higher revenues. So, the three classic goals of every professional service firm "service (clients) – satisfaction (staff) – success (partners)" are met if smart collaboration works in the practice.

Would Dr. Gardner's research be relevant also for a regional law firm headquartered in Austria with offices across Central and Eastern Europe? Remaining siloed along 10 practice groups and 13 offices was never an option; one of the firm's strengths has always been the ability to advise across borders and legal areas. But, approximately two years ago, we found that as everything, this could potentially be done even better, so we launched a project to foster smart collaboration at our firm. We invited Dr. Gardner to help us to understand the "why?" and the "how?" and launched a research project among our partners on the perceived barriers to collaboration.

Smart collaboration and mixing gin and tonics

But before we look into the project's details, let me explain what we actually mean by "collaboration" or "Smart collaboration," as Dr. Gardner calls it in her articles and her book *Smart Collaboration: How Professionals and Their Firms Succeed by Breaking Down Silos.*

Is it being supportive to each other and answering emails? Is it introducing each other's services to our clients? We have found in the practice that people often conflate collaboration with being cooperative or with cross-selling each other. However, the collaboration that really brings value is neither of these. Rather, it is a quality teamwork that is defined by diversity: "knowledge workers integrate their individual, specialized expertise in order to deliver high-quality, customized outcomes on complex issues". But we also found that to explain the difference and achieve change in the practice is not so easy – especially if you talk to busy partners. So, we needed a metaphor that is understood quickly and resonates well. Would lawyers understand smart collaboration if we explain it with the story of a gin and tonic?

Let's imagine that you are a gin expert bar tender. You have a deep knowledge about Tanqueray, Hendrick's, Martin Millers and the like. You are successful, gin is in. In the same bar, there is a tonic expert, Tom, a specialist in Fever Tree, Fentimans and Schweppes. He is not as much of a rainmaker as you are, but he is doing well. One day you notice that one of your best clients, Christy, is thirsty, so offering only gin will probably not be suitable this time (note: yes, you have such a good relationship with your client that you *notice*, she does not even have to tell you that she is thirsty!).

If you simply introduce Christy to the tonic specialist, Tom, that is cross-selling. She might skip the alcohol and not pay higher fees to any of you. Being nice and supportive to Tom is certainly not a bad idea, but the client does not care (and she is still thirsty). If the two of you – the gin specialist and the tonic expert – put your heads together, combine your knowhow and develop a gin and tonic, that results in higher fees (plus tips), in a satisfied client and in a fulfilling experience for both of you.

The benefits of smart collaboration

Let's go back to the office and look at why we need to put our heads together, not only as specialized bar tenders, but also as specialist lawyers. There are four main reasons why smart collaboration is essential:

1. Deep specialization and increasing complexity

Partners in "Big Law" firms have increasingly deep, narrow, and specialized expertise in their legal field. This makes it difficult for them to handle all of today's complex situations. Parallel to certain legal products becoming a commodity, there is a trend of increased complexity, resulting mainly from the globalization and regulation of business.

2. Increased fees, increased revenues, increased margins

Dr. Gardner's research has found that when more business units serve a client, revenues increase exponentially. Each practice area is better off when another joins the mix, as the complexity limits competition and keeps fees higher. As the main driver of the increase in revenue is higher fees, the margins also increase as teams collaborate to solve more complex problems.

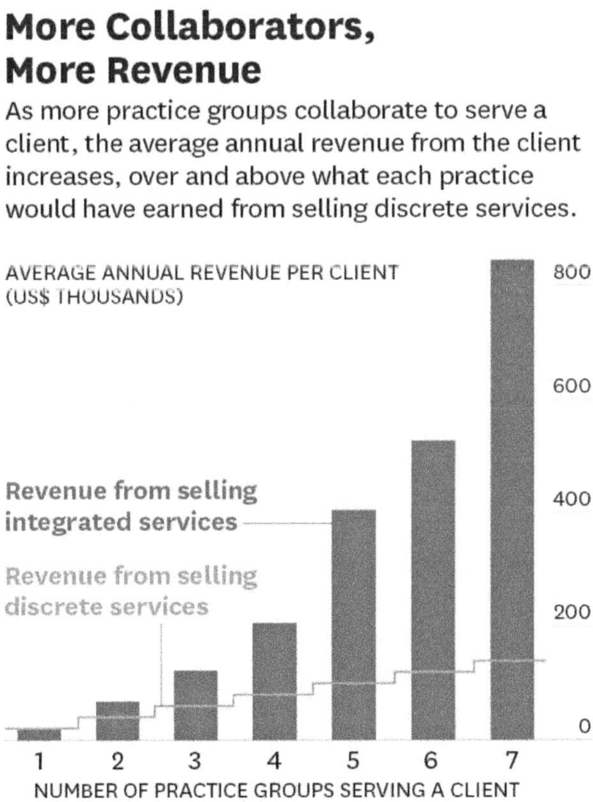

Figure 1: Cross-Unit Collaboration and Revenue. Source: "When Senior Managers Won't Collaborate" by Heidi Gardner, Harvard Business Review, *March 2015*

3. Higher levels of individual performance, higher satisfaction

The more robust the collaboration network of a lawyer is, the higher her individual turnover. More challenging, complex work, and more variety results in higher personal-professional satisfaction levels for individual lawyers.

4. Higher customer loyalty

Obviously, the more partners a client has contact with, the lower the likelihood that she will leave if one of those partners exits the firm. Multi-partner teams strengthen the relationship of the client *with the firm*, as opposed to having a relationship only with one lawyer.

Barriers to collaboration

When smart collaboration does happen, it is valuable for clients and fun for the collaborators. Revenues and margins are higher, individual performance is better, motivation is boosted by the variety of work, and client loyalty (apparently it exists!) increases. So, if it is a win-win situation and would make everybody happy, why don't we collaborate?

Perceived barriers prevent lawyers from collaborating. As mentioned above, right at the beginning of the collaboration project at our firm, we launched a research project among our partners on the perceived barriers to collaboration. Our results were very similar to Dr. Gardner's findings in connection with other firms. Similarly to many others, we also identified a tension between the growing need for collaboration and the value placed on individualism.

One of the main reasons is a knowledge management challenge. Apparently, lawyers have been digging themselves so deeply into their specializations that they no longer see each other's knowhow. They don't know about their colleagues' areas of expertise, trends, and new topics. They don't know what the others know. And they don't know what they don't know.

Another big barrier is lack of trust – trust that the other is able and willing to collaborate or that the process will be efficient. Instead of trust there is a fear that colleagues won't do good work, peers will take credit for others' work, and collaboration takes too much time.

Many don't trust themselves; they don't feel comfortable in addressing issues with a client that fall outside of their specialization, so they miss the opportunity to recognize collaboration opportunities.

Finally, as with every management problem, politics and messiness is a reason to underperform.

This is quite a long list: pick the one why you (sometimes) do not collaborate.

Steps to break down the silos

So how did we at Wolf Theiss start getting out of our silos and establish our strongest ever A-Teams?

1. Finding the ingredients (knowledge management)

In order to mix best-selling gin and tonics and other cocktails, we need to discover what ingredients we have. We have to learn what other teams and departments have as deep specialization, what hot topics and trends they see in their areas.

We have encouraged partners to meet each other more often at informal get-togethers, we have organized late-afternoon meetings (where we have even served gin and tonics!) and have asked partners to share views on legal trends with each other, with a strong focus on whether a product could be developed on the basis of cross-practice area collaboration. Practice Group Heads met for half-day-long workshops to talk about hot topics and developing joint client events, joint client newsletters and products to be offered directly to existing clients. Last, but not least, we have started to encourage lawyers to use Sharepoint and have created collaboration areas for cross-practice area topics (e.g. blockchain).

2. You get what you pay for (performance management)

One of the most important questions regarding fostering collaboration is whether it is incentivized by your performance management system. Is proactive collaboration – the inclusion of many specialists in complex cases, talking to clients and "hunting" in teams – a behavior that is positively rewarded at your firm, or does it measure success on an individual partner level?

In order to foster collaboration, we adjusted our performance management system, putting more emphasis on collaboration when target-setting and making remuneration decisions.

3. Finding success stories and celebrating the champions (change management)

To achieve change you have to recognize, communicate, and celebrate success on the path. It is especially true for change initiatives that address culture or a behavioral norm. Furthermore, you need to identify champions of change, demonstrate their examples and win them as change agents helping others.

So following the example of global firms, such as Herbert Smith Freehills, we have introduced for this year a Collaboration Point System to track individual partners' collaboration efforts. Our goal is to identify and celebrate collaboration champions in the firm, to emphasize that cross-practice area and cross-offices collaboration has more value than cooperating within their own legal field and own office, only.

We have asked partners to make notes during the year about fellow partners' collaboration efforts and at the end of the year distribute individually maximum 10 points to such other partners. Details of distributing such points have been laid down, e.g., there are no rules regarding what is considered as good collaboration, e.g., there are no requirements to charge on the particular matter, or there is no requirement to generate minimum fees by the commended act of collaboration.

Points will be awarded anonymously, but of course it is not forbidden to thank the other partner personally for her collaboration. At the time of writing the process is still ongoing, but we have already seen that, despite initial skepticism, partners are participating in the system.

4. Talking more to clients (client relationship management)

In the above bartender example, the challenge and opportunity to mix a gin and tonic starts with a client; Christy being thirsty. Similarly, everyday smart collaboration in law firms must also start with the clients. What are their business problems that could be tackled by several specialists working in a team? Good client relationships include frequent and targeted communication with clients with the aim to find out their complex business problems and offer them innovative solutions on the basis of smart collaboration.

First results

As Dr. Gardner points out, smart collaboration is about producing results, not just playing nicely together in the sandbox (although that's also important). It is still too early to tell whether long-term cultural change has already been achieved at our firm; also, financial results cannot be measured yet.

However, joint marketing projects, such as client events, newsletters, videos and press briefings where senior lawyers from different practice areas work together have risen dramatically. For example, client events where the speakers represent several practice areas and address an issue from these different angles has increased by 40 percent in 12 months. We also see that clients and journalists clearly prefer events and briefings that are based on smart collaboration compared to single-lawyer or single-practice area offerings. And, last but not least, our lawyers who have been involved in such smart collaborative marketing events or follow-up matters report that it is indeed a lot of fun putting together smart heads and mixing those gin and tonics!

Resources

Smart Collaboration: How Professionals and Their Firms Succeed by Breaking Down Silos by Heidi K. Gardner, PhD, January 2017
"When Senior Managers Won't Collaborate" by Heidi Gardner, *Harvard Business Review*, March 2015
"Getting Your Stars to Collaborate" by Heidi Gardner, *Harvard Business Review*, January 2017

Chapter 7:
Lawyer-led KM – a case study for mid-sized firms

By Harriet Creamer, director, Outer Circle

The question of how medium-sized and smaller firms respond to the challenge of establishing a knowledge management (KM) function which works for them has interested me for some time. Larger firms, with their seemingly limitless capacity for investment, have set the bar high. I spent the first portion of my career in the London magic circle, where funds can usually be found for anything that will drive the business forward, provided a compelling case is made.

These firms have invested significant amounts of money in both people and technology, and now have highly developed – and expensive – functions in place which underpin internal efficiency and quality and support the delivery of client service in new and innovative ways. In mid-sized and smaller firms, there is likely to be less of an appetite and capacity for investment, but the imperative for improving client service, both in terms of cost effectiveness and quality, is – if anything – greater than for the large firms. Increasingly, smaller, mid-sized firms are seeking to demonstrate that, at least in their chosen practice areas and geographies, they are a real and competitive alternative to the larger City firm.

The current KM landscape is very different from the landscape that existed when larger firms began to build their KM support functions. Considerably more sophisticated commercial KM provisions now exist than previously. While much of this is at a superficial level, for many firms it can take the place of at least some traditional internal KM functions. These include current awareness, some standard documentation (at least at a basic level) and, in some cases, initial analysis of new case law, statute, and regulation. This gives the smaller firm more freedom to develop a flexible KM infrastructure which meets its needs and allows it to compete effectively in an increasingly difficult marketplace, without requiring a significant internal infrastructure. Rather than copy the model adopted by larger firms, these firms can be more imaginative and focused in the KM solutions they adopt.

Smaller to mid-sized firms commonly have a further advantage over larger firms, in that they are more likely to have had some exposure to more "commoditized" practice areas and, in these practice areas, have been forced through greater competition and cost pressure to adopt ways of working not usually experienced in larger firms. By this, I mean both the use of computer-based case management systems and workflow products and the development of standardized, streamlined working processes which enable delegation to the least expensive resource.

My view is that a highly prioritized approach, targeted on those areas of practice to which focused KM can make the greatest difference, resourced largely through fee-earner involvement and supported by effective use of internal technology and external KM resources, is the way forward for the smaller to mid-sized firm. But, this approach works only if fee earners understand the need for change, agree priorities and are prepared to engage.

Over the last few years, Outer Circle has worked increasingly with firms in the small- to medium-sized bracket, helping them to reassess their approach to KM. This case study is based on this work, although some of the details have been changed to ensure that individual firms cannot be identified.

Assessing firm needs

A typical assignment will invariably begin with an assessment of firm needs. This starts with management. It is crucial to understand, from the outset, where the firm is and where it wants to be; its quirks and characteristics, its ambitions for its clients and the competitive landscape in which it operates.

This assessment is supported by a detailed analysis of the firm's financials, to identify the most and least profitable areas of the firm, based on its reported figures and write-off levels, as well as those areas where management perceives the greatest risks. We might also look at team profiles, time recording practices and other metrics the involved firm captures and feels may be relevant. We will interview a range of business support staff to get their take on how things work and the quality of the data we have been given. Importantly, too, we look at business plans – where these exist – and talk to fee earners about their aspirations for their practice area, the challenges they face, and the needs of their clients.

From this, we can build up a picture of the firm that guides our assessment of its needs and the areas of its practice where targeted KM initiatives are likely to have the greatest impact.

Partner engagement

At this point it is important to take a step back and look at management appetite for change. Typically, the firm's ambition will be to make the most of any existing KM resources without adding to them. At most, it will be prepared to contemplate additional investment only in targeted areas for which a very clear business case can be made and that will ideally impact positively on more than one practice area. If real progress is to be made, it will require effort and engagement from individual lawyers. Management needs to be serious about its commitment to better KM practice for this to be effective. Without wholehearted management support, it will be impossible to agree on and implement the practical steps which will be needed.

We will usually, at this stage, suggest intensive engagement with partners. Ideally, we will kick this off at a partners' meeting, where we put forward the case for a more effective approach and explain the lawyer-led one that we recommend the firm adopts. We will follow this up with focused sessions with practice and sector group partners where we can explain in more detail what this approach means for them.

We will also usually suggest the firm identifies a project lead at partner level, who can champion KM in the firm – not just for the duration of the project but also going forward. Our experience is that if a new approach is to be embedded in the practice of the firm it needs board-level oversight.

Working with the business plan

Not all the firms we work with have a clearly articulated business-planning process and may not have business plans, either at all, or across all their practice areas. If this is the case, we will work with partners to tease out at least their ambitions for the firm and its practice areas and put together a basic SWOT analysis, either for the firm as a whole or for the practice area concerned. Where there is a business plan, we will make sure that all the work we do is clearly focused on this. This gives vital context for all the KM projects the firm decides to undertake. In our experience, the greatest risk – and the situation in which we most often see KM fail in law firms – is where the KM function is divorced from the needs and imperatives of the business. Very quickly, in these circumstances, KM is sidelined and seen, at best, as an activity that makes only a limited contribution to business success, and, at worst, an expensive irrelevance. All KM activity must be seen to be aligned with and supporting the firm's business priorities.

Maximizing and incentivizing lawyer resources

Almost every firm will find that some of its lawyers are already thinking about how they can use their experience to develop smarter ways of working. Typically, they will be doing this more or less in isolation, on discrete projects aimed at delivering efficiencies only in their own practice area. At most, they may have involved other members of their group. Through interviews and discussions with key partners and others, we will aim to identify these individuals and encourage them to share the work they are doing more broadly around the firm. In this way, we help the firm build up a network of "knowledge pioneers", who can work with the KM project lead to champion the way experience and expertise can be channeled into new, more efficient, ways of working.

It is worth at this point saying a few words about lawyer incentives. In the UK – particularly in larger firms – it is finally becoming, if not common, at least less unusual to incentivize behavior beyond immediate fee generation and delivery of client work. In many firms, contribution to other business areas, including participation in KM activities, is being included in the matters reviewed as part of the appraisal process. Although we have not yet come across any firms which take non-fee-earning contributions into account in salary progression, an increasing number are taking this work into account in bonus allocation.

However, it is still the case that the most powerful incentive is partner behavior. If partners are seen to buy in to the benefits that effective KM can deliver, and both model and value good KM practice, other fee earners will be incentivized to follow suit. By adopting some of the techniques suggested in this chapter around targeted KM initiatives, based on work already being done and clearly aligned with and supporting the priorities identified in the business plan, the benefits of effective KM are more likely to be understood by the partnership in general. Partners are then more likely to encourage good KM practice by other staff.

Targeted initiatives

Having established our team of pioneers, we will help the firm prioritize areas where focused KM intervention will deliver tangible benefits. Ideally, this will result in a handful of projects which combine "quick wins" – where straightforward changes in practice can generate returns in the short term – and longer-term interventions. For maximum impact, the list should include a mix of internally- and externally-facing projects. We will usually work with the firm to draw up a list of KM priorities, based on the firm/practice area business plan or the SWOT analysis that we will have carried out by this stage (see above). This will identify:

- The issue that needs to be addressed – for example, quality, pressure on fees, lack of resources, specific client demand or perceived competitive threat;
- The proposed KM solution;
- The resources likely to be required;
- The anticipated outcome;
- How success will be measured;
- The timeframe in which this is expected to be delivered; and
- Who will take responsibility for delivery.

Where the proposed initiative is internally focused, we would expect the plan to identify the expected impact, whether this is supporting quality, minimizing risk or enhancing efficiency and maximizing profitability (or, in some cases, reducing loss). Where it is externally focused, we would expect the emphasis to be not just on enhancing client service but also on differentiation. In what way will the proposed project help the firm to stand out from its competitors and be seen to deliver something new or different to the market?

Examples of projects we have been involved in to date include:

- Projects that facilitate client conversations – for example (at its simplest), introducing an icon on the firm's intranet which links to a "hot topics" blog. Individual lawyers can post items on which they are currently engaging clients, which others can pick up. These might include changes in law or regulation of universal impact (for example, to rules around marketing and use of personal data) or changes that are likely to impact on a particular sector (for example, removal or reduction of subsidies in particular industries such as green tech);
- Projects focused on quality and risk management through expertise and experience-sharing, including the generation of practice-focused

"toolkits" for lawyers in specific practice areas. As well as helping to ensure that experience and expertise are shared, these are particularly valuable in cost-sensitive practice areas, enabling processes to be systematized and documents standardized, reducing the need for extensive input from senior staff without unacceptably compromising quality or increasing risk;

- Projects aimed at generating efficiencies, such as computer-based workflow products to develop an automated approach to matter management outside the more traditional areas of (largely) debt recovery, personal injury litigation and non-complex real estate work. This can work well, for example, for less complex private share and business acquisitions and in some financing transactions; and
- Projects intended to strengthen client relationships through the development of work tools which can be shared with the client, creating strong links between individual practice areas and the clients they support.

Technology

There is now a huge range of technology aimed at or adapted for the legal market. Much of this is expensive and out of reach of all but the largest firms. Currently, most of the products based on "artificial intelligence" technology fall into this category. These are increasingly being adopted by larger firms. Initially, use was restricted to client-facing applications, mainly focused around disclosure and due diligence, but, increasingly, their application to traditional KM functions (information retrieval and analysis) is being explored. While smaller firms may not yet be in a position to capitalize on these newer technologies, it is nonetheless worth staying in touch with developments.

In the short term, firms which cannot (or are not prepared to) invest significant sums in cutting edge technology can capitalize on more traditional law firm technology to deliver KM-based efficiency gains. We will engage with the internal IT team at an early stage. Invariably, the firm will already have access to technologies which can be harnessed as part of a KM initiative, if the IT team are brought on board. In our experience, the technical team are rarely included in business discussions and, once the firm's ambitions in terms of legal process efficiency and quality maintenance have been communicated, they are instrumental in identifying potential solutions based on the firm's existing technology.

For example, I have already referred to the possibility of exploring how case management and workflow products can be used beyond their traditional areas. Particularly when combined with document automation, these tools can deliver significant benefits in terms of cost-effective service delivery to clients, as well as delivering efficiencies to the firm while supporting quality and managing risk.

Typically, we will also be asked to look at introducing a new KM database or building on an existing one. In our experience, it pays not to take too ambitious an approach at the outset. We will work with individual practice areas to identify their most important subject areas and transaction or matter types, prioritize the collection of material in these areas and support the development of simple indexing protocols which will help to identify key features.

Working with PSLs

Most of the firms we work with already have a limited PSL presence. It is obviously very important to engage them at an early stage. They may find a change in approach both daunting and challenging – commonly, they will have had limited direction and will very much have built their own job description. While they may have communicated with other PSLs (inside and outside the firm) on law and regulation, it is unusual for them to have shared PSL practice. In this respect, our experience is that the KM function can be surprisingly siloed within firms.

Typically, PSLs work closely with individual partners who have a particular interest in a specific aspect of KM (very often around quality and technical skills). While the PSLs themselves may have begun to think about how they could support the business more effectively, they are unlikely to have explored this with the fee earners they work for. Frequently, we find they lack the confidence to do so and prefer to let the fee earners in their area shape their role.

We will usually suggest a program of PSL workshops, at which we share best practice from across the market and encourage the PSLs to share ideas and discuss both how these and broader market practice could be adopted more widely across the firm.

Our starting point is to help the PSLs engage with the firm as a business. While they may have a broad idea of its client base, in our experience time-poor PSLs are more likely to prioritize the traditional aspects of their role, which tend to focus on quality and risk (current awareness, standard documents and training) than on efficiency and profit. Their external focus, in terms of client needs, is again more likely to be on updating – producing newsletters and client alerts, mostly concentrated on legal and regulatory developments, and typically with limited practical content – than on improvement and innovation in client service. We encourage them to move away from the traditional aspects of the PSL role and think of themselves as facilitators, providing tools to fee earners which enable them to enhance their client relationships by delivering a high quality, cost-effective service, rather than solely as deliverers of legal and regulatory content.

Increasing PSL engagement at partner level can play an important role in PSL engagement with the business. We encourage partners to welcome PSLs at practice group partners' meetings and to engage them in the business planning process. This helps the PSL to understand firm and practice area priorities and encourages them to focus on where and how their engagement can make a real difference in terms of profitability. Building on this, we will help them to identify some key projects that individual PSLs (or, ideally, if there are several PSLs, pairs of PSLs) can take on. Not only does this approach give PSLs an insight into wider KM practice, but it begins to break down existing silos and foster a sense of a KM community across the firm.

Conclusion

The way forward for small- to mid-sized firms is to focus on the provision of prioritized KM activity, directed at identified needs and clearly aligned with the firm's business priorities, rather than to mirror the "full service" KM function in larger firms. The needs must be clearly stated and may be for efficiency in order to address a particular problem of fee pressure and low levels of profitability, for quality support and risk minimization (for example, in highly regulated areas where law and regulation evolve rapidly), or for differentiation in the eyes of clients in particularly crowded or competitive markets.

We recommend a "lawyer-led" model, where resourcing is largely focused on lawyers, rather than dedicated KM resources. This avoids the creation of an expensive infrastructure and allows the firm to flex its support, depending on priorities, but to be successful it requires real partner engagement and fee earner incentivization. Where dedicated resources exist, they should be focused on identifying where and how KM activity can support the firm's business priorities and on supporting and facilitating KM delivery by fee earners. Harnessing existing technology will be an important element.

Smaller and mid-sized firms, without the burden of a KM infrastructure built up over many years, are ideally placed to adopt flexible solutions which meet their changing needs.

Chapter 8: Matter-centric knowledge management at Stewart McKelvey

By Cyndi Murphy, knowledge manager, Stewart McKelvey

Lawyers think about and organize their work by matters. All of the work that a lawyer does for a client is stored, whether in paper file folders or electronically in email and document management systems (DMS), by the matter. For billing purposes, each matter is assigned a unique identifier to track time spent and costs disbursed. Using human and machine knowledge management tools and techniques, such as a consistent taxonomy, a centralized and intuitive user interface, and systems designed to use the same information in multiple ways, the information from those matters and about those matters can be leveraged to ensure law firm success.

Background

Stewart McKelvey is based on the east coast of Canada and ranks among Canada's top 20 largest law firms. With the appointment of a new CEO, Lydia Bugden, in 2015, the firm intensified its focus on innovation as the way in which the firm would position itself, both in the practice of law and in the business of law, to flourish in today's market and to continue to be profitable in the future. One of Lydia's initial appointments was Paul Saunders as the firm's first full-time practice innovation partner. The firm also created a Practice Innovation department and established the Practice Innovation Advisory Committee (PIAC). PIAC is a firm committee whose mandate is to provide input and advice to Lydia on the execution of five items which include, among others, implementing pricing analyses for various practice areas and ensuring regular reporting to the partners on Practice Innovation, including metrics on cost reduction and profit enhancement.

As PIAC began reviewing a number of aspects of Stewart McKelvey's business in order to try and improve systems and procedures and obtain more meaningful data on operations, committee members realized the truth of that old adage, "Garbage in, garbage out". There was lots of data being collected throughout the firm, especially by the financial accounting system, but it could not be applied in a meaningful way to the practice innovation projects. That realization resulted in the implementation of two specific knowledge management projects under the auspices of PIAC which were matter-centric – a consolidation of the matter types and a revamping of the client industry types, both of which are identified when a new file is opened.

At Stewart McKelvey, every file, or matter, has a unique identifier, consisting of two numbers separated by a dash (e.g. SM123456-00001). The first number, prefaced by the letters "SM" and consisting of six digits, is unique to the client. No matter how many matters the firm opens for the client, that number remains constant. The second number, consisting of five digits, is unique to the matter, and is assigned in numerical sequence as new matters for the client are opened.

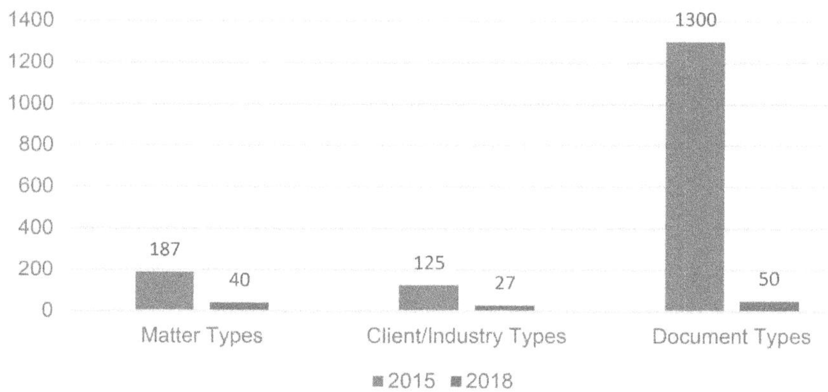

Figure 1: Making matter data meaningful

Matter types

Prior to July 2016, when a new matter was opened, there were 187 different matter types to choose from. Only 155 of those were being actively used. Within those 155 there was considerable overlap, making it hard to measure the amount of actual work the firm did in a particular area or which lawyer, office, or department did it. Accordingly, PIAC members worked to consolidate the list of matter types and reduced it to 40. The new matter types aimed for consistency of use rather than granular specificity. They mirrored the taxonomy developed previously for the organization of Practice Toolbox, a compendium of precedents, checklists, and sample documents on the internal portal, SMartNet, and reflected the major areas of practice in the firm.

In order to maintain a limited and consistent taxonomy, no new matter types can be added without the approval of PIAC. Since the consolidation, one new type, Aboriginal Rights, has been added, to reflect a growing area of practice in the firm that was not captured by any of the other categories.

Client/industry types

A year after the matter type consolidation, PIAC changed the client type codes used in the financial accounting system to better reflect the industries represented by Stewart McKelvey's clients. The change reduced the previous number of 125 codes to 27 – 26 industry codes, plus the code INDI, which was retained for clients who are individuals.

The North American Industry Classification System (NAICS) Canada 2017 was the basis for the new codes, but a few names were modified and a couple of categories were split apart to better reflect Stewart McKelvey's needs and its clients. For example, NAICS classification code 52 combines Finance and Insurance. Stewart McKelvey has many large clients in the financial industry and also has a large insurance defense client base. There is a Stewart McKelvey client type for "Finance" and a separate one for "Insurance". NAICS uses the term "Fishing"; Stewart McKelvey uses "Fishery".

NAICS is the standard used by Statistics Canada, so it is now possible to generate industry statistics and compare those with Stewart McKelvey's analytics. This information will be used for practice rationalization and business development. With fewer codes to choose from, it is easier to correctly identify the client's relevant industry and fewer separate categories of industries enables meaningful analysis for pricing purposes.

Document types

The next project on the continuum to rationalize and organize business data, in order to be more innovative in the practice of law, will be to review and rationalize document types. They will integrate with the organization of the matter types and be implemented when the firm switches its DMS to NetDocuments in 2018. NetDocuments stores documents and emails in matter-centric workspaces, so that functionality will be leveraged.

Currently, there are over 1,300 different document types, spread over six different networks (each office has its own document library) in the DMS. There is no consistency in the terminology used for the document types in each province, so there can be up to six different codes and descriptions for the same type of document. Although some document types are used consistently, some have been used fewer than 10 times since their creation. There are too many choices for a user saving a document, so the default is frequently "Miscellaneous" or "General", negating the benefit of assigning a document type as a field that can be used to retrieve documents of a specific type.

The goal of the document type project is to make it easier for users to find and collaborate on documents saved in the DMS. To that end, there are two priorities – to reduce the number of choices a user has when saving a document, and to tie the choice of document type to the matter type identified when the file (matter) is opened. Within the 41 matter types, document types that are meaningful to that practice of law will be identified. Some of the document types will be available across all matters (e.g. "Correspondence" or "Speeches, Papers, Presentations" or "Precedents"). Other document types will be unique to the matter type (e.g. "Share Certificates" for securities matters or "Mortgages" for real property matters).

When a user saves a document in NetDocuments, the document types available will be presented as a limited option, determined by the type of matter on which the lawyer is working (Figure 2).

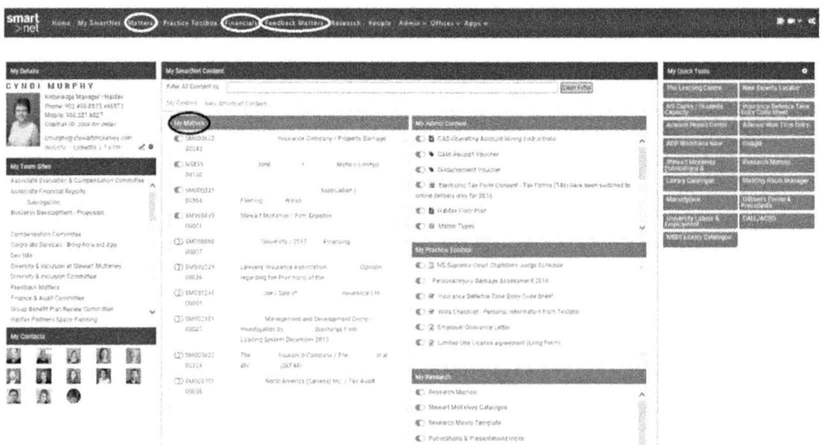

Figure 2: Limited document types in NetDocuments when saving

At Stewart McKelvey, matter-centric knowledge management is not limited to the compilation of financial data. The Sharepoint portal, SMartNet, was designed to be primarily matter-centric and the just-released performance management system, Feedback Matters, relies on matter information to generate data.

SMartNet

Before he became practice innovation partner, Paul Saunders had a vision for a Sharepoint portal that included matter-centric information integral to a lawyer's practice of law. Handshake Software enabled the firm to implement his vision.

On the portal, SMartNet, in the My Matters section, it is possible to see a list of all matters on which a user has saved time in Aderant, the financial accounting system, authored a document in the DMS, or has been the sender or receiver of an email saved to the email management system, Decisiv. Choosing a matter from the list, the user retrieves information about the file, for example. the name of the billing lawyer and when the file was opened, as well as a list of all documents saved to the file, whether the user authored them or not and all emails saved to the file, whether the user was on the distribution list or not. A user has the ability to open any document in the list and edit it in the DMS, or print it, or open any email and reply or forward it. Because most of the legal assistants are in teaming situations, they see the names of the lawyers they support through a pull-down list that allows them to choose the specific lawyer whose work product they want to access. Any user can filter the lists by document number, title, author, document type and date for matter documents, sender, RE: line, and date for matter emails. It is also possible to keyword search across all fields in either category. My Matters content appears on the personalized My SMartNet page of the portal and there is also a link on the menu bar at the top of every portal page.

Even if a user has not been involved in a matter, it is possible to locate file information in the All Matters section by searching on the client and matter number or name or a combination of the two. As long as the matter is not behind an ethical wall, or the documents have not been assigned a high level of security, anyone can access all of the information that the user would have had, had the matters been in the My Matters list. It is also possible to tag matters and move them to a My Matters list. This functionality is particularly helpful for associates who are being brought onto a matter after it has been open for a while. For example, looking at previously created documents and emails

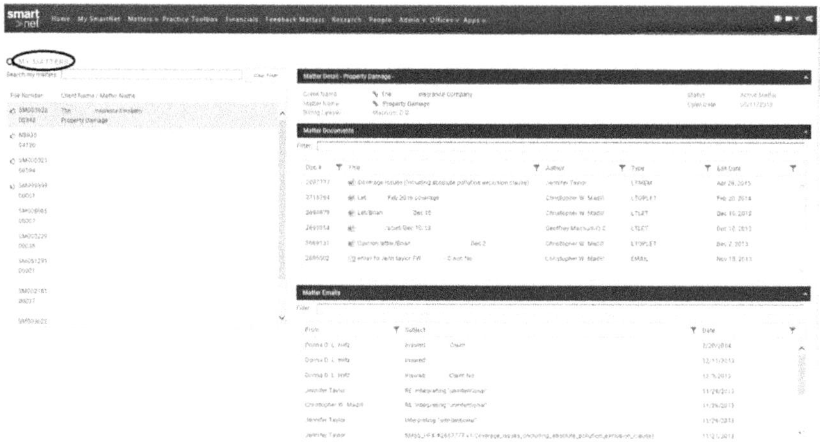

Figure 3: More efficient searching to make research more relevant

enables the associate to get up to speed quickly and easily before a client meeting. The articled clerks and summer students also find it useful. When they are asked to do research on a matter, they may not be given all of the facts of the file, or information on previously conducted research. Searching all matters and scanning the list of documents and emails often provides the context necessary to make their research relevant (Figure 3).

The Financials section of SMartNet provides a billing lawyer with details on WIP, AR, Trust Balance, Fees Billed, and Unapplied for any matter for which he or she is responsible (Figure 4).

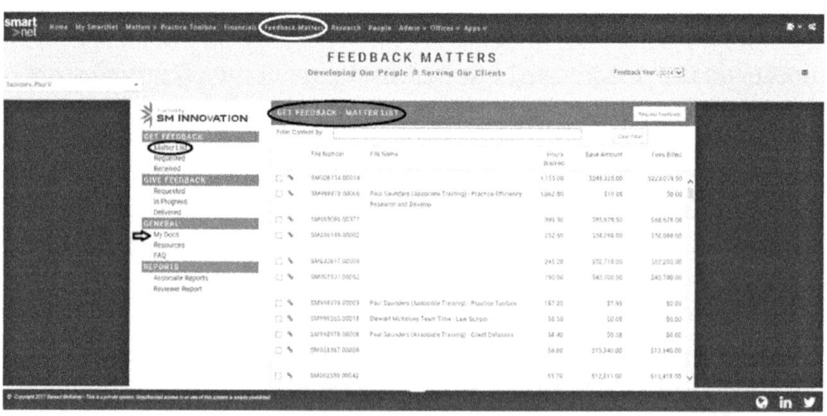

Figure 4: The Financials section of SMartNet

Feedback matters

We tend to think of matter-centric knowledge management as developing infrastructure to collect information about things, but understanding the information about the people providing client service in the law firm is just as important, or more.

In September 2017, Stewart McKelvey launched Feedback Matters, an application developed in-house using Handshake Software and leveraging the knowledge gained throughout the development and enhancements of SMartNet. Designed to provide just-in-time (as opposed to once-a-year) feedback to associates, Feedback Matters, accessed through a tab on SMartNet, organizes data by matter. It facilitates regular access to constructive feedback and easily compiles performance feedback for annual review and advancement discussions, as well as compensation decisions. Associates can request feedback on a matter and view the feedback given. Partners can respond to requests for feedback, or initiate feedback on a matter. The associate is prompted to fill in a description of the work for which he or she is soliciting feedback. The partner is prompted to fill in information under the headings "What Worked and Why?", "What Didn't and Why?", and "Focus Areas". Among other information in Feedback Matters, for easy reference, there is a link to the documents the associate has authored on a given matter.

Feedback Matters was developed in direct response to comments from associates and partners about their pain points in the previous way by which Stewart McKelvey conducted associate evaluations. Once a year, partners were asked to provide comments on the work done for them by associates during the annual review period. Partners could not remember specifics about work done for them, so comments were general and not constructive in providing examples of ways in which the associate could improve, or continue to do what the associate was doing well. If there was a specific example, it tended to be a negative comment rather than a positive one, made several months after the fact, so the associate felt there had been no opportunity to discuss the issue with the assigning partner, fix the mistake, and avoid making it in subsequent client work.

With Feedback Matters, associates can solicit, and partners can provide, feedback in real time to make it more actionable and meaningful, thereby driving the development of Stewart McKelvey's people and improving client service. Matter-centricity is at the heart of Feedback Matters since that's how lawyers think about and organize their work.

Conclusion

The matter data is at the core of every lawyer's practice and Stewart McKelvey's knowledge management and practice innovation teams are continually looking for ways to leverage that data to make decisions about the firm's practice of law and the firm's business. Using the same taxonomy for the SMartNet Practice Toolbox and the matter types provides consistency and enables the linking of document types to matter types, ensuring fewer choices, and consequently more likelihood of making the right choice and providing meaningful data. Using a client type taxonomy that mirrors NAICS enables Stewart McKelvey to compare its financial information with objective, third-party statistics. The SMartNet portal puts all of the electronically stored matter-specific information in one place and the ability to personalize a user's main page means the matter information most relevant to the user is only one click away. Information stored in the accounting and DMSs can be analyzed for people development, for practice development, and for business development.

Chapter 9: New organizational value brought about by AI technologies

By James Loft, CEO, Aigen

In this chapter, I will focus on the concept of 'value' to organizations and their ability to tackle challenges and opportunities created by complex (and often restricted) working environments through the application of artificial intelligence (AI) technologies, and therefore creating enriched and in some cases creating new value to those businesses.

Value is a subjective and often contentious topic. I define value as a characteristic of achieving something that offers an improvement or new opportunity related to a characteristic of a business, such as customer satisfaction, operational efficiency, taxation and profit creation, through to regulatory and governance standards.

In order to specifically think about this in relation to knowledge management (KM), I would like to take it further and characterize it as the value that organizations want to get out of their knowledge and how to best position themselves to reap the benefits of it working for them.

Making more from what we already have (new knowledge from old)

Often when exploring the application of organizational knowledge, the first place organizations start is reviewing what we already have. The purpose is to create a format or structure that can be used to gain insights and useful features from the knowledge in order to somehow understand or enhance the activities that are carried out day to day.

In order to do this, we tend to build two things. Firstly, we build some sort of ontology or taxonomy of what we have, either through a list of document types, previous experiences, services, or the skillsets of team members. We then build sets of rules around those structures, some of which are imposed upon us, others of which are self-imposed in order to maintain consistency or quality. Often, these two elements are not separate entities as I described, but are rather captured in large amounts of unstructured text-based descriptions and manuals, which tend to be placed in digital format on intranets, searchable guides or knowledge hubs.

There is a simple and obvious problem with this. The high-value knowledge gets lost, whereas the old or outdated knowledge remains. This means that as our customers, colleagues or clients become more used to receiving information in a bespoke way, we are struggling to keep up.

In this instance, AI brings new value, in that it is not as easily bound by these traditional elements and has the capabilities to make the crucial switch between unstructured and structured knowledge in order to better offer up this value. This is coupled with the benefit of not having to start from scratch or create new interfaces for accessibility, as this AI technology takes the existing information in its current format.

A further creation of value to consider here is that once the data has been consumed, technologies that are reading and mapping knowledge have the ability to provide visibility and insights into the information that previously wasn't easily available or hidden. This is often due to the sheer volume of knowledge available within organizations that has built up over time and is a symptom of a well-used product or service. This capability is not just being able to find knowledge that you had lost sight of. Instead, it provides you with the opportunity to hold the entire knowledge base in your hands and to combine knowledge in new ways to create new knowledge from what exists, which can be extremely valuable to organizations.

So, why can new value be achieved from what is already known? Many organizations have recorded and structured their knowledge and information, and there are a myriad of tools and techniques to capture that on an organizational level, which requires huge investment and should not be lost or overlooked.

This is best described as the automation of new knowledge patterns from a vast ocean of knowledge. There is the opportunity to accelerate this further with the addition of codified human knowledge in order to make decisions from the organizational knowledge, both in real-time and at scale. Up to this point, you required humans alone to deal with this, or had a machine trying to do so in a robotic way but reaching a point where high volumes of anomalies are a matter of course.

With this in mind, take a large bank or retail firm as an example of where rules and procedures are documented in order to be used by remote staff members in bank branches and shops in a consistent way. It is often the case that this is supported by a comments section where colleagues can share the easiest and preferred methods of dealing with situations, yet the documentation is not updated to reflect the advice on how to best carry out specific tasks. Sharing information in this way adds value, but such organizations are struggling to reflect updated knowledge in the legacy systems that have been adopted, which has led to an overwhelming amount of knowledge being created and shared, but no way of managing this knowledge to create a single source of truth.

Making automated decisions – at scale

Think about the most knowledgeable person in your business. By "knowledgeable," I mean the best trained and most liked by customers across the entire organization. Now imagine that person is readily available in your pocket or on your desktop to support you every second of everyday, without going home at 5pm, getting in late, taking a day off sick or handing in their notice. Not only would you get support with the right way of doing a task, you would get it immediately and with the situational factors that you are facing factored in so as to ensure that you're giving the right answers to your customers or colleagues.

This isn't a matter of imagination, however. In order to do this, we need only to think about two new things. One is the interface, and the second is the existing technologies that are required to support this offering. However, to confess, the new interface is not new at all. In fact, it is the fundamental way in which humans seek information in order to gather information and converse in the right way. It is, however, new in terms of being able to get an answer from a collection of unstructured or verbose information. I am, of course, referring to chat as an interface.

Humans use chat to explore topics. The ability to quickly ask and answer questions is how humans establish context in the written or spoken format and how we achieve an element of bespoke information when we require it. The exploratory nature of a conversation ensures an agreed level of contextual understanding and when we refer to a breakdown of communication it is often this interaction that is lacking.

There is nothing more infuriating to us as humans than trying to engage in a conversation when the other party does not expand or share information to support context gathering. The commonly quoted "computer says no" is due to the common experience of an organizational expectancy that a conversation will be able to evolve to a point of clarity or resolution on a topic, but an organization's approach limits this. We want to be supported in the conversation by the other party and have expectations of what that support looks like.

A chat interface is a good way of using a tool that has a recognizable structure from a human's perspective and can interact with us rather than providing a solitary answer. This is where we need to start looking at the technologies required to achieve the results we desire. In order for an automated system to work like a human, we need a system that thinks like a human (often a non-data led interaction, full of instinct and context-swapping), so that a system's understanding can go beyond the data available to start understanding the way in which a human brain works in relation to language and its application, rather than physiological traits. I am referring to a system that has the ability to understand and replicate the theory of decisions and language as a way of determining a goal or task.

So, do humans make decisions? This is the logical starting point, and the concept of inference is critical to understanding how we go about decision-making ourselves.

If I were to give you a number of facts about my friend Gary, I would then expect you to be able to infer further things from the facts presented with a level of confidence, based on how much I tell you. You won't actively think about it this way but you will weigh up what I tell you in order to build up a better picture of Gary.

For example, here are some facts about him:

- Gary lives in France; and
- I happen to know that the national language of France is French.

From this, we can derive a number of elements. Firstly, that Gary is a person and France is a country. On top of this, I have also told you that Gary lives in France; therefore, you know people live in a country. Then we can look at some of the relationships in these facts, so in this example we can see that a country has a national language and that the instance of the national language for France is French.

Armed with those two pieces of information, a natural inference (or joining of the dots) could be achieved if, when I ask what language Gary speaks, you might say "French", because he is a person who lives in a country which has French as a national language. That, in principle, is the most basic element of inference. I could add additional facts for you, such as that the country someone was born in has a larger impact on the language that they speak than where they live, so with that in mind, and having not told you where Gary was born, you might want to ask me that question in order to enhance the certainty of your response regarding the language that Gary speaks.

If you allow your organization to record and hold its information in such a way, you are immediately opening up new opportunities for how questions are answered at scale and how a natural, human-led approach can be used to provide bespoke answers for every customer in a unified and controlled way. This AI technology is often referred to as 'cognitive reasoning', but is best thought of as an automated decision-maker and is one of the leading types of AI for the more complex end of the operational scale for businesses. Technologies for this kind of offering have two approaches. The first being driven by machine learning processes which set out to achieve a similar outcome by using past interactions in order to predict the right one to suggest in a new interaction, and the second is based on a human-down approach where you capture the knowledge of humans and codify it into a tool to scale that individual's expertise to the business.

Making everyone in your organization a specialist

With the ability to scale the complex element of decision-making comes the added value of being able to serve your customers more immediately, or at least to give them an enriched experience at the first point of contact.

First-line resolution is not a new concept for organizations, especially those who have complex or high-volume front-line teams. AI, through its ability to offer clarity in large swathes of information, however, brings the reality of achieving it one step closer through the ability to highlight relevant support and salient advice for people to use in real time while an interaction is occurring.

Imagine a call into a customer services desk where the phone system goes one step further and listens to the call, identifies what the agent is being asked for, and gathers a bespoke response from a knowledge bank of information, pinpointing the exact paragraph where the solution has been identified, ready for someone to read out. Then imagine the enhanced version of this where the answer is spread across five paragraphs on three different pages, but the system collates the information and writes a script for the phone operator to read out, taking each of those relevant elements into account.

This complex process of entity and intent extraction is hugely powerful when you take into consideration how it empowers your staff and improves the customer experience. The ability to write a bespoke script uses this extraction from the data and then applies a technique called natural language generation where it turns disparate elements of knowledge into a consistent piece of prose that is appropriate to be read out aloud to a customer.

The real value here is creating a consistent and uniformed offering using AI technologies to do the job currently carried out by a highly paid or highly valued specialist or second line teams at a level that increases the consistency and quality of your front-line team and empowers them to not need to research a solution to your question or find a specialist as a customer waits for them. It also empowers the customer-facing team to focus on building up a customer relationship and deliver a highly satisfactory customer experience, rather than getting distracted to look into various databases to find and collate a relevant answer.

So, what does that look like as a set of value creations for a company? Firstly, you have a higher customer satisfaction, because they are getting information in a timely manner, which feels like a bespoke or specialist piece of information or advice that has been gathered quickly and efficiently. Then, you are getting the opportunity to reduce the number of people in the second line and specialist team's due to the new scalability of the knowledge that you have provided to the front-line staff, giving your front-line the power to be proxy specialists to customers. Finally, you get consistency and uniformity in the expertise provided which provides high customer satisfaction, which in turn means that there is a lower turnover rate within the first-line team because they are dealing with happy customers.

Such benefits are driven by a customer response that is derived from a signed-off process with supporting documentation having been written by the organization rather than the individual, leading to a massively reduced risk position while increasing efficiency.

Where a 'colleague assistant' such as the one described has been used, it is often well received by front-line teams and seen as an enabler for success rather than a job security challenge due to the ability to provide a higher level of value to the customers, making the team look better, as well as the ability to return to their core skill of relationship building, rather than data entry and sourcing.

The final added value that such systems offer to an organization over traditional mapped approaches is the ability to grow. It enables an organization to expand content rather than being limited by a need to rebuild a new element every time something changes, as would be the case in rigid systems or a decision-tree based approach.

If a regulation changes, pointing the system at the new wording will search in relation to the latest source information and will therefore be immediately up-to-date in relation to the guidelines. This is a process that can be rerun against previous questions and information provided in order to highlight potential customer impacts that would occur from changes taking effect.

Supporting remote- or safety-critical environments with the best knowledge

If a company's information can be on everyone's desktop, it means that you can make decisions in an automated and – ultimately – scalable way, and we can start to look at some of the applications of such AI systems. One environment to take into consideration is a safety-critical or engineering environment where approval or sign-off is often needed as a process where the actual work is carried out in specific, restricted or remote places. Imagine a scenario in which you are decommissioning an offshore oil field, or repairing a remote section of railway or road late at night – there is a safety or environmental impact of getting something wrong, not only to yourself but to other people, as a consequence of failing to do the right job.

Value in this circumstance is the ability for a worker or team leader to have every specialist in their pocket by capturing the details of what they are doing and how to go about carrying it out correctly and safely. It is easy to think about knowledge-sharing in a warm office environment, but it is also required elsewhere. Due to limitations, it is often hard to provide without a large cost or delay to what is being done. For example, the current version of the scenario is to send a safety person, a quality inspector and an environmental specialist to the location, or to have them on call in order to provide the necessary support.

Time and location are a major constraint in the traditional approach but this can be alleviated by capturing these specialists' knowledge in a tool so that their knowledge is always readily available to answer questions that are fixed and procedurally driven, but also to react to the specific circumstances and changes of the environment as they are neither linear nor bound to the risk profile of assumptions made in a planning approach. Such a "cognitive reasoning" system would add value here in a different way because, by the very nature of inference, the system will only return answers if it has been able to establish the outcome with a confidence level that the author is happy with, and therefore it has an additional capability which is the ability to ask what it doesn't know. If further information is needed to ensure that a situation is safe, it will continue to ask questions in order to understand the context of the situation better and increase the confidence level to provide an accurate response. As such, this audit or interrogation style approach supports situations such as these where a large number of factors play a part.

The way in which the questioning is carried out by the system is determined by what is deemed to be the most appropriate and relevant way in order to reach an answer with a certainty level that is above the set threshold. Therefore, it is not easily tricked or bypassed by a user who, by default, increases the quality of the output or adequately identifies where further work or remediation is required. If a concern is raised, then it can remotely offer up the outcome of the decision for review, including the information provided by the user for checking and validation purposes.

This engineering situation is one of many examples and looks at the situation of a planned change with checks and balances required. However, the same systems approach can be applied through a similar approach to accounting or professional services, or more reactively in audit and security environments.

Seeing more than people can, including into the future

So far, the value discussed has been largely related to the human element of what an organization knows and how to bring new meaning and scale. It is important to note that data is an equally powerful prospect. We should think about what Donald Rumsfeld once referred to as the "known unknowns" to truly understand this value. By this, I mean the value through data or information that is buried in your organization and not recognizable (and therefore is not usable) by humans, due to its volume.

The ability to miss minor patterns in large amounts of data has, on a number of occasions, been heralded as the reason for financial crashes, due to the size and complexity of the data presented to us. Small numbers of data points in a sea of others are easily lost or not understood with their true value in mind. Having the ability to understand, enrich, map and begin predicting future value from data has a huge impact and is not achievable without AI-based technologies to support.

The word "prediction" is often used in this machine learning and general analytics space to offer up some kind of magic recipe or crystal ball, but, in essence, it is the identification of often hidden micropatterns or patterns only seen when you compare new elements of data together that can then start to shine the light on a path from the past to a current point and therefore provide insights into a trend which can be pushed outwards in order to see what is likely to happen next.

If you have the ability to show what the data is actually telling you – for example, what your customers actually think of you in a customer satisfaction sense, as well as identifying some of the human elements present in the data, such as emotional intelligence from happiness to fear, and apply it to the metadata – then you can start to see some truly emotionally intelligent situational elements of behavior and show movements to predict behaviors as an outcome of those shifts.

Knowledge for everyone in the organization

In the knowledge management environment, the ability to understand a collective or complete view of what the organization knows is a huge challenge and one that often sees high value capability and knowledge walk out the door. Some of the new AI technologies are creating the opportunity to democratize knowledge, and are starting to make what is known across the business available to the entire organization. This is powerful to an organization on the highest of levels, as learning and experience are being maintained and shared with a wider group of people, sometimes even after the original source of the knowledge has either moved on or does not have the ability to directly share the information across the organization.

However, there are also benefits in the short term for organizations that build new, scalable knowledge that tackles the silos often seen today. There is an opportunity to share knowledge across business units or teams, and for each element to benefit from an easily accessible view of how the wider team groups work. This remote approach to sharing is a good fit for geographically disperse or purposely separated teams as it allows the best of all skillsets to be shared across the entire organization.

This ability to take part in someone's knowledge or expertise and share that element across the organization is an interesting perspective and is starting to be seen in how new start-ups are challenging traditional markets. They are using AI to bring modules together to create an ultra-bespoke user experience. A recent advancement in the physiotherapy marketplace is a tool that builds bespoke services of patient-specific activities to be offered to the patient based on a short initial interaction. The knowledge for each of the specialisms is recorded in text and videos across a range of activities, which amounts to the knowledge of an entire team of specialists, and the user receives a bespoke program based on the elements they require with input from all of the specialists. By providing feedback, the support that they receive is continuously refined and varied through effort required or type of activity, all based on the advice of a collection of the best specialists.

User-based knowledge and interactions

As a final thought, we should focus on how this new knowledge and improved ability to scale decisions really supports the end user, either through the ability to automate and therefore remove complete steps in friction-filled processes, or to switch interactions to asynchronous communications that never end.

Removing pain points is an important element and follows a design-thinking approach to interaction design that has been present for some years. The basic principle of not taking someone through something if they don't need to be engaged reflects approaches such as progressive disclosure, but can remove entire elements of processes for them with automation as a driver. Often invisible to the end user, these automated processes can be anything from listening in to phone conversations with operational teams and turning call details into pre-filled application forms, through to fraud automations that can better identify triggers for processes such as blocking credit cards.

Asynchronous communication is a shift in how people interact with each other, especially in the UK, where text forms a large percentage of how we interact. The interest in having open-ended conversations with individuals is starting to progress towards how users want to and expect to interact with organizations. Traditional web-based chat interfaces have extended the reach of companies to speak to more clients in a way that better suits them, but they are still powered by people and are not scalable without great expense.

AI can help some of these organizations open up elements of this type of communication. Firstly, the ability to always be truly available and secondly to take information regarding the reason for contact and previous interactions to set proper context and therefore best serve customers. Imagine being able to text your meter reading to your utility company and getting the response, "thank you for your reading," and being able to respond weeks or months later with a question about your usage, such as, "how do I reduce that?" and the system answers immediately while taking into consideration who you are, your circumstances, and the relevance of what "that" means from the last communication. These interfaces and the technology that powers them are just as important as the technology itself.

Conclusion

We have seen a few AI technologies that have the ability to add new and real value to organizations brought to life with some real-world examples, all of which are in production today in some form. The value elements I mention are not new types of value, but they do increase the ease of achieving them and are accelerators to traditional attempts that have been explored many times before with little success. Some are simply elements that have not yet been attempted, whilst some are still being assessed for the challenges that face organizations.

This chapter has set out an exciting opportunity position relating to what is possible. It describes elements that can act as accelerators to success across a number of different businesses and at scale across departments within them. New technologies, in particular AI, will continue to advance. In a matter of months, such a chapter would have had to include a whole new set of systems that add value in this space, but the speed of creation for applications to businesses are levelling out and the outcomes are clearer and demonstrable now more so than ever before. These are not new technologies of the future, they are value-giving tools for today.

www.ingramcontent.com/pod-product-compliance
Ingram Content Group UK Ltd.
Pitfield, Milton Keynes, MK11 3LW, UK
UKHW021848150926
8657IPUK00005B/147

9 781783 583126